Emma Phipson

Choir stalls and their carvings

Examples of misericords from English cathedrals and churches

Emma Phipson

Choir stalls and their carvings
Examples of misericords from English cathedrals and churches

ISBN/EAN: 9783741140075

Manufactured in Europe, USA, Canada, Australia, Japa

Cover: Foto ©Andreas Hilbeck / pixelio.de

Manufactured and distributed by brebook publishing software
(www.brebook.com)

Emma Phipson

Choir stalls and their carvings

CHOIR STALLS

AND THEIR

CARVINGS

EXAMPLES OF MISERICORDS

FROM

ENGLISH CATHEDRALS AND CHURCHES

SKETCHED BY

EMMA PHIPSON

AUTHOR OF "ANIMAL LORE OF SHAKSPEARE'S TIME."

WITH AN INTRODUCTION AND DESCRIPTIVE NOTES.

LONDON:

B. T. BATSFORD, 94 HIGH HOLBORN.

1896.

CHOIR STALLS AND THEIR CARVINGS.

PREFACE.

IT is no exaggeration to say that there are thousands of misericord carvings in English cathedrals and churches, yet many people are quite unaware of their existence. The fact is that the majority of travellers do not see what they are not told to look for, and guide books rarely mention these seats; sight-seers, therefore, daily stroll through the choirs, turning neither to right nor left, because their attention has not been called to the carvings. In one cathedral I remarked to the verger that, judging from the dust, the seats had not often been raised, "No," he said, scornfully, "Who wants to look at the horrible things?"

It seems strange that no work has yet appeared dealing exclusively with these old carvings, rich as they are with their wealth of myth, beauty, humour, and antiquarian interest. In most of the choirs of our cathedrals we find a range of fifty or sixty carved pictures, in which weird creatures, unknown to science, such as "Alice in Wonderland" would have loved to meet, are seen in conflict, in repose, or in amicable converse with human beings. The prototypes of the *Jabberwock*, the *Jubjub*, the *Griffin*, and the *Snark* can all be traced in these quaint forms; we see groups of men and women pursuing their daily occupations, each dressed "in his habit as he lived," forming a gallery of mediæval costumes; and what is, perhaps, more interesting to the modern craftsman, the groups are frequently enriched with sprays or bosses of foliage, in many cases exquisitely carved.

The best account of misericords is by Mr. Thomas Wright, F.S.A., in *Essays on Archæological Subjects*, 1861, with numerous illustrations, and *History of Caricature in Literature and Art*, 1865. Some seats were engraved and described by John Carter in his *Specimens of the Ancient Sculptures and Paintings now remaining in this Country, from the Earliest Period to Henry VIII.*, 1780; and Mr. Llewellyn Jewitt contributed a series of papers entitled "Art under the Seats" to the *Art Journal*, 1875, fully illustrated. Descriptions of misericords in some cathedrals and churches have been published separately, but they are for the most part very difficult to procure. The series in Worcester Cathedral were described by Mr. Noake, and published with excellent photographs, by Mr. Aldis in 1873. Beverley Minster and Ripon Cathedral have been fully described, with illustrations, by Mr. Wildridge, of Hull, and those in Bristol Cathedral by Mr. Leversage.

With regard to the drawings, allowance must be made for the very awkward position of most of the carvings; sometimes, as at Ely, the seats are placed so low that it is necessary to crouch on the ground to see them. The "dim religious light" of many churches puts another drawback in the artist's way; at St. George's Chapel, Windsor, for instance, where the carving is very elaborate, the gloom is proportionately profound. Owing partly to this absence of light, and partly to the ravages of time, there is often considerable difficulty in making out the intention of the carver. It may be noticed that occasionally there is a variation in the drawing of the same misericord by different artists, just as several explanations are sometimes given of illegible handwriting. It is necessary to interpret the meaning of a group before beginning to sketch it, and, having made up his mind what is intended, the artist will unconsciously make his drawing agree more or less with his interpretation of the subject; while another spectator will put a different construction on the carving before him, and his drawing or explanation will vary accordingly. For instance, one authority explains a misericord at Norwich cathedral as representing the Prodigal Son feeding swine; another thinks that it depicts a woman pursuing a fox who is running off with a goose!

I may point out that the apparent difference in the size of the seats is mainly due to the shape of the bracket, and the presence or absence of "supporters" or side ornaments; the back line of the seat is in every case the same size.

The greater part of the descriptions of the seats have been supplied to me by Mr. Thomas A. Martin.

The subject of misericord carvings is so extensive that the first attempt to deal with it as a whole is likely to be very imperfect. The meaning of many of the groups still remains to be explained by antiquaries well versed in mediæval lore. Mr. Thomas Wright truly remarks that these sculptured stalls, besides their value for the study of manners and costume, form a practical illustration of the kind and degree of scientific and literary information it was thought necessary to place before society at large; consequently, an extensive study of the literature of the Middle Ages is needful in order to understand the objects of art those Ages produced.

In the present volume several cathedrals and many churches are omitted for want of space; and some counties, especially in the north, are quite unrepresented. I hope, however, to supply some of these deficiencies in a second series, and shall be greatly obliged for any corrections or suggestions. I shall also be grateful for information respecting places where these carvings occur which are not included in the topographical list at the end of the volume, which I am anxious to make as complete as possible.

I venture to appeal to clergymen, architects, and others interested in church restorations not to allow these relics of early art to be thrown aside when they are removed from their present position. If there is no part of the church where they can be conveniently placed, they might at least be sent to the nearest museum, or to the Architectural Museum at Westminster. A few of these carvings have been rescued during the process of "restoration," and deposited in safe quarters by considerate antiquaries, but a large number have been irretrievably lost. When the seats in the church of North Cadbury, Wilts, were handed over to the contractor and found their way into the timber-yard, Mr. Reynolds, of Gainsborough House, bought them and gave them to the well-known carver, Mr. Harry Hems, of Exeter, who has carefully preserved them. Others have probably been purchased by owners of country houses, and utilised as hall seats. I shall esteem it a great favour if anyone possessing these carvings in their halls or chapels will permit me to see and describe them.

5 PARK PLACE,
   UPPER BAKER STREET,
      LONDON, N.W.

CONTENTS.

B

CHOIR STALLS AND THEIR CARVINGS.

INTRODUCTION.

"THE seats you are now passing are very remarkable for their carving," intones the custodian of Westminster Abbey, as he conducts his band of sight-seers through the Choir of Henry the Seventh's Chapel; but if anyone stops to examine some of the extensive series, he is politely requested to keep up with the party, and has to hasten on; and, indeed, to appreciate the beauty and interest of the range of carvings would take a much longer time than the custodian's patience would tolerate. The object of the present volume is to draw the attention of those who have the opportunity of travelling about England, to these interesting works, which are almost entirely ignored by guide books. When studied collectively these carvings become of far more value than when examined singly, as we are then able to compare them and to trace their development.

The choir is the part of the cathedral or church on which, as a rule, most attention was bestowed; the richness of its ornamentation was limited mainly by the diminution of funds in hand. A choir stall was a most important and elaborate portion of church furniture; it consisted of (1) a misericord, or folding seat; (2) a book-desk, or *prie-dieu;* (3) the parclose (the lateral pillar or partition, the upper carved part forming the *museau*); (4) an *accoudoir*, or elbow-rest, which, as well as the misericord, gave support to the occupant of the stall when standing, and forms the division between the stalls which generally terminated in carving (the elbows of Winchester Cathedral are specially fine; (5) a *dossier*, or panel at the back; (6) a *baldaquin* (a canopy or tabernacle) of open-work carving, often extremely rich and beautiful

in execution.   Tabernacles and canopied backs superseded the curtains
and draperies which were first used to keep out the cold.

These stalls are found in mediæval cathedrals and also in churches
attached to collegiate or monastic and charitable institutions.   Their
seats are frequently of a moveable character, and are made to lift up
on occasion ; the seats in a modern theatre, which can be raised to
make room for passers-by, are an adaptation of this idea.   They worked

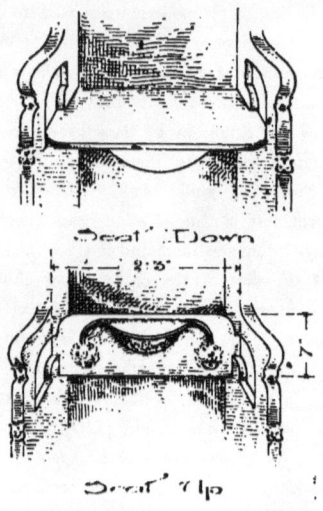

on hinges or pivots, and underneath they had a kind of bracket, which,
when the seat was raised, formed a slight support to persons in a
standing attitude.   As the Rev. E. F. Letts observes : " Our prede-
" cessors must not be considered lazy, because they allowed some
" slight assistance to tired limbs.   The ancient offices of the Church

" to be said daily were seven, *Lauds, Prime, Terce, Sext, Nones, Vespers,*
" and *Compline,* besides, of course, the daily Celebration (often more
" than once) of the Holy Eucharist. . . At each of these offices
" four psalms, besides canticles and hymns were recited; $4 \times 7 = 28$
" $+ 7$ canticles $+ 7$ hymns $=$ 42 standings to sing daily, besides endless
" versicles and responses."—*(Misereres in Manchester Cathedral.)*

These seats are known by a variety of names; misericords, misereres,
subsellæ, sellette, and sometimes they are called "nodding-seats," from
a popular notion that if the occupant, during a long service, was inclined to sleep and bent forward, they fell down with a bang! French
archæologists call them *misericordes* or *patiences,* and the Italians, *pretellæ.*
The seats are now seldom raised, but it is easy to imagine that, when
they were all uplifted, the effect would be a bold band or frieze of
carving, which would add great richness to the appearance of the stalls.

It has been supposed by many that the carvings on these seats
were intended as a satire by monks on the secular clergy, on rival
monastic bodies, or on the mendicant friars; others contrive to see a
deep symbolic meaning in every group. It certainly seems strange
that such direct attacks upon clergy of whatever body should have
found admission into a place of worship, but the early church was
wise enough to encourage talent of every kind which could contribute
in any way to the enrichment and attraction of her buildings, and
strong enough to tolerate occasional ridicule of her ministers, especially
as the caricature was personal, and in no case doctrinal. Some ecclesiastics, indeed, inveighed bitterly against the introduction of similar
grotesques into a church. St. Bernard of Clairvaux, in an "Apology"
addressed to William, Abbot of St. Thierry, in the twelfth century,
expresses his indignation very strongly. "What is the use," he asks,
" of that ridiculous monstrosity placed in the cloisters before the eyes
" of the brethren when occupied with their studies, a wonderful sort of

" hideous beauty and beautiful deformity? What is the use there
" of unclean apes? of ferocious lions? of fighting soldiers? of hunters
" sounding their horns? Sometimes you may see many bodies under
" one head; at others, many heads to one body; here is seen the
" tail of a serpent attached to the body of a quadruped; there, the
" head of a quadruped on the body of a fish. In another place appears
" an animal, the fore-half of which represents a horse, and the hinder-
" parts a goat. Elsewhere you have a horned animal with the hinder-
" parts of a horse; indeed, there appears everywhere so multifarious
" and so wonderful a variety of diverse forms, that one is more apt
" to con over these sculptures than to study the scriptures, to occupy
" the whole day in wondering at these, rather than in meditating upon
" God's law." The pious writer concludes: "For God's sake! if people
" are not ashamed of the extravagance of these follies, why should
" they not, at least, regret the expense required to produce them."—
The Archæological Album, edited by Thomas Wright, 1845, p. 91.

The best explanation of their presence is that given by Oliver Baker
(*Ludlow, Town and Neighbourhood*). "Great difference of opinion exists
" as to the meaning and purpose of these carvings, but it seems from
" the character of them that, at a time when pictures were few and
" the power to read rare, they were the *genre* pictures or story-books
" of the middle ages." They also afforded an opportunity of introducing portraits of local celebrities, either the Bishop or Prior, or
some benefactor to the church, but it is, unfortunately, impossible at
this distance of time to identify the likenesses. As the stalls were
generally appropriated to a particular office or benefice, it is likely
that the design of the carving may, now and then, have an allusion,
more or less direct, to the habits or propensities of the occupant of
the stall in which it was placed.

The ornamentation of these seats forms the subject of our present inquiry. It varies considerably in detail, but is all of the same general character; the carving which supports the bracket generally represents a subject, sometimes a single figure, sometimes a group. From the moulding of the bracket on each side springs a side-ornament, which occasionally refers to the central group, but has frequently an independent subject. These side-ornaments, to which the heraldic name of "supporters" is sometimes given, are very often foliage, which for the most part corresponds with the style of foliage decoration in stonework of the same period in the church.

The ledges or bracket-seats of misericords vary greatly in shape and mouldings; some are perfectly flat, some are hollowed, some have a smooth slight curve, others have sharp angles. Their date can often be ascertained by these differences; the curves of the bracket-moulding, sometimes called cusps, finials, or roundels, take endless variety. Sometimes, as at Exeter and Chichester, the "supporters" come close up to the seat; sometimes the moulding lengthens out and encloses the "supporters" in medallions, as at Manchester and Beverley, or twines in long tendrils round them, as at Lincoln and St. Margaret's, Lynn.

Occasionally the "supporters" are dispensed with altogether, as at Gloucester. The front of the moulding is now and then enriched, as at Beverley, with small arches, and at Lincoln with tiny roses. The workmanship varies as much as the subject. Mr. Letts, in his very interesting notes on the series at Manchester, finds traces of three separate hands: "the first one, who is *facile princeps*, is noted for his " *scenes;* his figures, whether human or animal, are extremely good, " and he gets in all the details in a truly wonderful and comprehensive " way. Each group tells its own story, and the more you look at " them, the more you see in them; the under carving is wonderful. " The second carver delights almost exclusively in *fabulous animals,* " which are often most ingenious and grotesque, but neither in delicacy

" of finish nor originality of conception can he be compared to the
" first.   The third hand is evidently that of an apprentice ; the subjects
" are clumsy attempts to copy the second carver's beasts, but the work
" is far rougher, and the anatomy and proportion very inferior, and
" not worthy to stand side by side with the first carver's results."   At
Chester, again, Mr. T. Cann Hughes *(Chester Archæological Journal,*
vol. v., p. 1, 1893) discovers three distinct workers, of varying excellence,
possibly the same men.   At Ludlow, some of the seats have a dis-
tinguishing mark, an incised cutting of a conventional sprig ; no doubt
the private mark of the artist.   At Exeter, some of the seats are
marked with circles, either the mark of the workman, or the ·mere
diversion of an apprentice.

The foliage which is introduced into many of these carvings is
extremely graceful and well executed, especially in the earlier examples
at Exeter and Winchester.   It is unfortunate that the size of the
accompanying drawings is on too small a scale to do more than give
a suggestion of their beauty.

The period in which misericords are found extends through several
centuries.   The earliest known series is at Exeter, and dates from the
thirteenth century.   In the fourteenth and fifteenth centuries they were
very frequently introduced, and the workmanship was at its best.
George I., when he revived the Order of the Garter, added seats in
St. George's Chapel, Windsor, and in Westminster Abbey, to provide
accommodation for the extra number of knights, and in our own time
these seats are occasionally added, though the use for them no longer
exists.   Many examples have been lost by the ravages of fire and time,
a great number were wilfully destroyed by fanatical zealots, while some
were removed from their original position at the time of the Dissolution
of monasteries, but their worst enemy has been the modern "restorer."
In numerous cases these interesting relics of antiquity have been

taken away during the process of renovating the choir, and instead of
being sent to the local museum, have been handed over to the contractor
and have found their way into timber yards. J. Carter, in his fine
work *Specimens of Ancient Sculpture in England*, published in 1787,
describing the church of St. Katharine by the Tower, writes thus :—
" This church, with St. Bartholomew the Great, St. Mary Overy,
" and the glory of Gothic architecture, Westminster Abbey, are all
" we have remaining of this city's ancient religious splendour ; the
" present rage for extirpating every vestige may soon, alas! reach
" these sacred piles." His gloomy forebodings were soon realised, for in
1825 the church was pulled down to make way for the docks which bear
its name, and only a portion of its treasures have been preserved in a
small church, built in connection with St. Katharine's Hospital, in the
Regent's Park. A collection of casts of misericords and a few originals
are now in the Architectural Museum in Tufton Street, Westminster.

    The chief home of misericord carvings is in the Eastern counties.
In Norfolk not only the important ecclesiastical buildings, but even
the village churches have these ornaments, and in the south, Kent is
particularly rich in them. These carvings were chiefly the work of
Flemish artists, who came over in the reign of Edward III., and
settled in the Eastern counties. Bands of workmen were often attached
to a church, and went from place to place as occasion required. They
were probably specially trained for this work, and were well versed in the
legends and traditions of their time. The same workmen, for instance,
were engaged on the wood-work of St. George's Chapel, Windsor, King's
College, Cambridge, and Westminster Abbey. These were chiefly
Italians, under the superintendence of Torrigiano, a Florentine artist,
pupil of Michael Angelo. He made an attempt on his master's life,
which, fortunately for art, was not successful. He fled to England to
escape punishment for the assault, and won the favour of Henry VII.

c

and his successor. There is very little foundation for the popular theory
that these works were executed by the monks, although it is possible that
occasionally a recluse may thus have employed his leisure time.

To fully understand the meaning of these carvings the student
must compare them with every other form of decorative work of the
time. Similar subjects are found depicted in the stained glass of the
windows, in the stone carvings of the spandrils, gurgoyles, and capitals
of pillars, also in the brasses, and in the tiles or mosaics of the
floors of ecclesiastical buildings. Calendars, missals, and even the
books used in the services of the church were profusely ornamented
with subjects of a similar character.

A very noticeable feature in these carvings is the strong sense of
humour which pervades them, though the humour differs considerably
from that of modern times. Many of the "gestes" and "merrie tales"
which so delighted our forefathers, provoke in us only wonder that
they afforded any amusement at all. Preachers frequently aroused the
attention of their hearers by anecdotes and illustrations which in our
time would not be considered seemly. The old mysteries and miracle-
plays were a strange compound of moral teaching and broad humour;
comic incidents occur in the same scenes as the most solemn and
tragic events ; the Devil is invariably the comic personage of the piece,
although the lesson to be drawn from his interference in human affairs
is serious enough. In the moralities, the mirth-maker of the piece is
the Vice, or Iniquity, who was usually carried off by the Devil at the
conclusion of the drama, and, according to Strutt, "in compliance
" with the old custom, Punch, the genuine descendant of the Iniquity,
" is constantly taken from the stage by the Devil at the end of the
" puppet-show."—*Sports and Pastimes*, book iii., chap. 2.

It must be remembered that our ancestors were very realistic, or
rather, literalistic, in their art, and, if they wished to represent the

Spirit of Evil, had no hesitation in portraying the Devil as they imagined him to exist. Though we may smile at the mode of execution, the lesson taught is a solemn one. For instance, a demon with out-spread wings and eagle's talons, chasing a naked figure, represented the pursuit of a lost soul; the doom of the wicked was frequently shown by these lost souls being forced by the demon into a monster's wide-open jaws, the conventional method of depicting hell-mouth. This conveyed a forcible truth to those to whom the idea of eternal punishment was a vivid belief. Mediæval painters treated these subjects in a similar way; the demonology of misericord carving throws great light, not only the nature of particular subjects, but also on their specific aim and purpose, and it further, in some degree, explains much of the teaching intended to be conveyed.

The chief source from which the subjects of these carvings are taken was the "Bestiaria," or Books of Beasts, that is, books of living creatures in general. They were natural, or rather, *un*-natural, histories of animals, so treated that the peculiarities of each beast should convey a wholesome moral. In the middle ages these books were very popular, and furnished materials for sermons.

The Landseers of the period may have obtained their models from the private menageries, which were not uncommon, though they do not appear often to have availed themselves of the opportunity.* The first English menagerie was at Woodstock, in the time of Henry I. It contained lions, leopards, and other wild animals, and was transferred to the Tower of London in the reign of Henry III. There the

---

* In the *Facsimile of the Sketch-book of Wilars de Honecourt*, an architect of the thirteenth century, first edited by M. Lassus and published in Paris, but afterwards translated and edited by the late Professor Willis of Cambridge, there is a remarkable study of a lion, which is so grotesque a representation of the king of beasts, that one reads with incredulity the inscription "This is a lion as he is seen when viewed in front, " and take notice that it was drawn from life."

collection remained until it was superseded by the establishment of the Zoological Gardens in the Regent's Park.

Other sources were fables, after the manner of Æsop, and satiric Beast Apologues; the most important of these was the satire of Renard the Fox. The long satirical poem of *Reineke Fuchs* first appeared in the twelfth century; portions of it had been written two centuries before, and in the fifteenth century it became universally popular. The latest version is a satire on the state of society in Germany during the middle ages; the plot turns chiefly on the long struggle between Reineke the Fox, who typifies the Church, and his uncle, Isengrim the Wolf, who stands for the feudal baron; Nodel, or Noble, the Lion, who is no less carnivorous than the others, represents royalty. Reineke is swayed by a constant impulse to deceive everybody, whether friend or foe, especially his uncle Isengrim; and though the latter frequently reduces him to the greatest straits, he generally makes his escape in the end. In the Bristol misericords, no less than nine carvings appear to be taken from this work. In one of the seats, Renard is about to be hanged for his misdeeds, and the King, Queen, and courtiers assemble to witness the execution. Renard invents a tale of some hidden treasure which he promises to disclose if his life is spared. Other incidents, equally amusing, are depicted. The Fox appears also in another guise: habited in ecclesiastical vestments, placed in a pulpit, and preaching to geese or barn-door fowls. He is sometimes accompanied by his friend the Ape, who stands behind him with geese slung over his shoulder, or peeping out from his cowl. Places where these preaching foxes occur will be found in the Subject List. According to a writer in *The Sacristy*, vol. i., ii., this symbol was designed to act as a warning to the preacher not to flatter his audience or to seek to make profit out of them, and to warn the people that flattery and profit-seeking are the marks, not of a true apostle, but of a deceiver.

The use of animals is very frequently symbolical; they are often intended to represent a moral characteristic, otherwise untranslateable in wood. Almost every saint had an animal as his or her peculiar attribute; St. Mark had a lion, St. Anthony a pig, St. Giles a hart, &c.

The intense love of nature, and the religious feeling of the Gothic mind, was embodied in the various departments of decorative art. Mr. James Fowler attributes a mystic import to most of the representations. The course of the sun through the zodiac, he says, had an important significance; it represented the course of the Sun of Righteousness through the festivals of the Church, which marked the divisions of the ecclesiastical, as the signs of the zodiac did the divisions of the natural year. Each apostle originally presided over the sign of the zodiac and labour of the month during which his festival fell. The universal belief in the influence of the planets and stars on human life would doubtless be reflected in artistic work. This suggestion of symbolic significance gives additional interest to the productions of mediæval art, but it will not do to push the theory too far, as it would be very difficult for a carver to choose any subject, however familiar, from the rural life around him, which could not be endued with a "mystic import;" besides, some of the subjects, such as milking and spinning, can scarcely be limited to one particular month. Mr. Fowler gives a description of subjects peculiar to the different portions of "the ever-running year" at Worcester, Malvern and Gloucester. The order is necessarily conjectural, owing to the re-arrangement that has taken place at various times. He has also drawn up the following table of symbols employed here and in other places.

JANUARY. Ploughing. Pouring water out of a vessel, for *Aquarius.* A drinking-horn, with the mouth turned to the left, for the prolongation of the feast; the same, turned to the left, to show that the Christmas festivities were over. A pruning-hook, or grafting-knife. A two-faced figure, seated behind a table, feasting. Wavy lines, for water. A man carrying wood. Lifting a pail from a well. Watering the ground. A woman in a hood and cloak, spinning. Man in tall peaked cap, sitting, warming his hands over a fire. Man digging. *Janus*, seated, drinking from two cups. *Janus*, closing one tower and opening another; the Old and New Year.

FEBRUARY. Pruning trees or vines. Fish, for *Pisces* and the fishing season. Felling trees. Man warming himself. Digging. Sowing.

MARCH. Digging. Sowing. *Aries*, a ram. Full-faced sun. A hut, with an ox's head, to show that oxen still require to be tended before going out to grass. Weaving. A tree in leaf. A barrel, for March ale. Goat browsing. An armed warrior, for *Mars*, carrying a shield, on which is depicted the lion of St. Mark. Blowing a trumpet, for wind. Man breaking bough off a tree. Man blowing two horns, his hair streaming behind him. Shepherd blowing pipe. Sheep-tending. Man and hawks.

APRIL. Bull, for *Taurus*. Ship, for navigation season. Tree, budding. Tree, in full leaf. Cuckoo. Cow and calf. Birds singing. Pruning. Roses. Sheep and lambs. Nests.

MAY. Twins, for *Gemini*. Sheep and lambs. A large bird, for hatching-time for domestic fowls. Small bird, for hatching of small wild fowl. A fish. Milk-pail. Hawking. Roses.

JUNE. Reaping. Sheep-shearing. Fishing for salmon and pike. A turnip. Weeding. Mowing. Eight-legged creature, for *Cancer*. Vine leaves. Making a barrel. Cherries.

JULY. Felling trees. Hay-making. Fruit. Acorns. Lion, for *Leo*. Gathering grapes. Threshing. Weeding.

AUGUST. Mowing. Reaping. Female figure, for *Virgo*. Hops. Stag-hunting. Threshing. Barrel-making.

SEPTEMBER. Boar-hunting. Scales, for *Libra*. Apple-gathering. Sheep-shearing. Flocks of birds, for migration. Threshing. Grapes. Slitting a pig. Crushing grapes. Squirrel and acorns. Catching small birds.

OCTOBER. Hawking. Eight-legged reptile for *Scorpio*. Wool-carding. Harrowing. Making wine. Acorns and pigs. Cutting wood. Threshing. Digging.

NOVEMBER. Centaur, for *Sagittarius*. Acorns and pigs. Goose, for Martinmas. Ploughing. Sowing. Sow and pigs.

DECEMBER. Threshing. Iron staff, for walking on ice. Sledge. Can of beer, for St. Ann. Weaving. Two horns, crossed, for Christmas. Head of a goat, wings and tail of dragon, for *Capricornus*. Cutting wood. Warming at fire. Pig-killing. &c.

Archæologia, vol. xliv., 1873.

The early carvers were fond of dealing retributive justice in their works. At Manchester there is a group which has been called "the hare's revenge," which represents a huntsman bound hand and foot to a pole in front of a roaring fire. Over the fire hang some pots with lids. A hare raises the lid of one of the pots, and discloses the head of a hound who is being stewed. At Malvern the rats are represented hanging their old enemy the cat. At Sherborne and elsewhere the fox is being hanged by geese. In this class must be included the numerous scenes where women are shown as inflicting chastisement on their husbands.

Employments of every kind are represented; a very interesting example of a wood-carver in his workshop was in St. Nicholas, Lynn, but is now in the Tufton Street Museum. The carver is seated at a bench, his dog at his feet, measuring the pattern on a piece of wood; further on two assistants or apprentices are engaged in carving, and other specimens of their work stand behind them. The "supporters" are apparently initials, pierced with a saw and a gouge, the implements of his craft. Carvers at work occur also at Wellingborough and at Brampton.

Hawking and hunting scenes are not uncommon; sports and games occur occasionally, as well as domestic incidents of various kinds, such as cooking, spinning, and even quarrelling. At Beverley and Lynn a man is wheeling a scolding wife in a wheel-barrow, probably to the nearest pond. Mr. G. Oliver amusingly describes a scold as "one who has merited distinction by her superior powers of eloquence "and the facility she possesses in adapting tropes and figures of "rhetoric to every occasion and circumstance of common life " (*Hist. of Beverley*, p. 328). Rural incidents, again, make a pleasing change from the fierce combats between knights and dragons. At Beverley there are some charming groups of a cat and her kittens and a hen with her brood. Legends and stories from mediæval romances were probably often introduced, but the great similarity in the narratives of encounters between heroes and giants, lions and other adversaries, makes it difficult to ascertain the authority for the scenes. For instance, Siegfried, the hero of the *Niebelungen Lied*, and St. George, vanquished a dragon and rescued a fair princess ; Samson and Richard I. must divide the honour of inspiring the numerous carvings of men astride lions, rending their jaws, apparently with the utmost ease. A belief in dwarfs, trolls, pixies, and underground workers in mines was prevalent in these days. In German legends Alberic, the King of the Dwarfs, with his cloak of invisibility, may be the origin of some of the gnome-like figures with large heads and crafty countenances which often form the subject of these carvings.

Angels, human figures, and even animals are often represented playing musical instruments ; a sow playing the bagpipes while her young ones dance to the melody occurs frequently; at St. Katharine's Hospital an angel is performing on one of these instruments, which certainly does not suggest celestial harmony. The wandering minstrels and troubadours who had at one time been very popular, began, in the fourteenth century, to lose favour, and were often made the subject of satire. They mostly played the harp; fiddle, or viol; bagpipe; pipe, single or double ; the tabor, the ancient name for the drum ; cithern, an early form of the guitar and the hurdy-gurdy. Over the altar at Gloucester Cathedral there is a series of angels in full choir, with every instrument of music played in the fifteenth century. Some of the forms are very curious.

Heraldic decorations, coats of arms, &c., are often found, and were probably intended to immortalise some contributor to the church funds.

Compound animal figures, or combinations of human and animal figures, such as are described by St. Bernard, are found chiefly in the earlier carvings. Mr. Moncure D. Conway explains these monstrosities to be "a kind of crude effort at *allgemeinheit*, at realisation of the "types of evil—the claw principle, fang principle in the universe— "the physiognomies of venom and pain detached from forms to which "they are accidental." (*Demonology*, vol. i., p. 319). It is probable that in these grotesques a symbolic meaning underlies the artist's imagination, but some of them may illustrate mummers and their doings.

Acrobatic performances were very popular, and tumblers in every variety of impossible attitude are found. The ancient story of "My Lady's Tumbler," shows the favour in which these performances were held. A member of a monastic order, who had once been an acrobat, had none of the talents of his companions, had yet a strong spirit of religious fervour. He was one day discovered by his superior in a quiet nook going through a series of elaborate performances in tumbling before an image of the Virgin, and he continued his exertions till he fell exhausted on the ground. Then, to the surprise of the Prior, the figure stretched out her arm, and restored him to his accustomed vigour. This miracle was reported to the other monks by the Prior, with the remark that the man whom they had been inclined to despise had displayed greater devotion than any of them. From this time the monks used daily to watch from behind a curtain, unknown to the supple-limbed brother, for the recurrence of this miracle. In a misericord representing the death of John the Baptist, at Ely, the daughter of Herodias is represented as tumbling, not dancing. In a version of the scriptures in the eleventh century, it is said of Herodias's daughter, "she tumbled and it pleased Herod," as if the translators imagined that no ordinary dancing could have earned so great a reward.

D

Scripture subjects are of rare occurrence, strange to say. As in the paintings of the time, the figures in these scripture scenes are always represented in the costume of the day; every accessory, every association, being those with which the carvers were familiar. For instance, in a carving in Winchester College Chapel, the Good Shepherd is represented, not as a young man carrying a lamb as if it were made of cotton wool, with a sanctified expression, as a modern artist might represent him, but as a regular " Hodge," protected against the weather by a cap tied under his chin and huge boots, grasping his woolly charges with an uncouth tenderness which may suggest burlesque, but which was certainly not intended for it. One of the finest scripture scenes is " The Judgment of Solomon," in Westminster, a most elaborate piece of carving.

Among the most interesting subjects are some local ones, such as the salmon at Christchurch, the swan and her cygnets at Windsor, the plover and woodcock at Higham Ferrers, and the beaver carrying a branch in its mouth at Worcester.

There are many subjects that defy any explanation whatever, which were probably due to the mere fancy of the carver at the moment.

All the characteristics which Ruskin ascribes to Gothic architecture are to be found in these quaint carvings, namely :—

1. SAVAGENESS.—The wildness of imagination and roughness of work peculiar to the northern nations are here, frequently coarse and unrestrained, but the direct expression of the artist's thought.

2. CHANGEFULNESS.—While the general plan is adhered to, the variety is so infinite that, although we sometimes find a subject repeated, the treatment always differs. The few cases where exact repetition occurs are due to the employment of an inferior artist to complete the series, probably at a later date.

In later times monotony appears to be considered a beauty; for instance, it would have been impossible for the artisan of the Gothic period to have produced thirty-six seats all exactly alike, such as we find at Lincoln College, Oxford (1660).

3. NATURALNESS.—Most certainly we find here "the love of " natural objects for their own sake, and an effort to represent " them frankly, unrestrained by artistical laws." However rough the workmanship may be, the characteristic of each animal is carefully preserved. The foliage, also, though not a servile copy, is evidently taken direct from nature. " Both Greek and Roman " used conventional foliage in their ornament, passing into some- " thing that was not foliage at all, knotting itself into strange " cup-like buds or clusters, and growing out of lifeless rods " instead of stems; the Gothic sculpture received these types, " at first, as things that ought to be, just as we have a second " time received them; but he could not rest in them. He saw " there was no veracity in them, no knowledge, no vitality. Do " what he would, he could not help liking the true leaves better; " and cautiously, a little at a time, he put more of nature into " his work, until at last it was all true, retaining, nevertheless, " every valuable character of the original well-disciplined and " designed arrangement."

4. GROTESQUENESS.—"The grotesque is in almost all cases " composed of two elements, one ludicrous the other fearful. . . " There are few grotesques so utterly playful as to be overcast " with no shade of fearfulness, and few so fearful as absolutely " to exclude all ideas of jest." The humour which pervaded every department of art and literature in the middle ages is seldom absent from these carvings, even when the subject is a serious one.

5. RIGIDITY.—There is often a certain stiffness and lack of grace arising from the energy of the worker.

6. REDUNDANCY.—The very existence of misericords illustrates the enthusiasm which could decorate profusely a portion of the woodwork so often hidden from view.

Stones of Venice, vol. ii.

The Rev. Charles Boutell, in a learned paper which was intended as an introduction to a work on misericords, which, unfortunately never appeared, points out that " in a variety of ways these carvings constitute " illustrated chronicles of the personal history of the English people. " The accuracy and truthfulness of these chronicles are attested and " confirmed by the fact that they were written by men who were " altogether unconscious of being chroniclers at all. These early artists " used their chisels, not to record, but to instruct, to warn, to encourage, " to guide, to beautify, and to criticise. They worked under the " impulse of motives altogether devoid of the historical element. They " were influenced by the traditions of their art, by their own feelings, " and were directed by their own knowledge, experience, and observation, " and also by the associations of their every-day lives. It follows that " if we would read the old chronicles aright, we must as far as possible " identify ourselves with the chroniclers. We must look at their works " from their point of view, and not from our own. Our object must " be to endeavour to discover what they intended to convey, to " investigate the means and appliances at their disposal, and to " familiarise ourselves with what they knew would be understood, and " therefore would be expected from them."*

---

* This introduction is now in the MSS. room of the British Museum.

CHOIR STALLS AND THEIR CARVINGS.

DESCRIPTIVE NOTES.

The Letters " D. & S." refer to the *Dexter* and *Sinister* Supporters.

EXETER CATHEDRAL.

The misericords here are of great interest, as being the earliest series now preserved; they date the middle of the thirteenth century, and were probably executed in the time of Bishop Bruere, 1222-1244. They have all been cut away to fit their present position; they were re-arranged at the time of the restoration of the choir in 1874. The "supporters" are generally well-executed conventional trefoil foliage, and are rather small. There are fifty stalls with misericords; ten are returned, five on each side. An account of these carvings, by Mr. Harry Hems, of Exeter, with illustrations, appeared in the *Building News*, for December 4th, 1885.

North Side, commencing West.

1. Fine spray of raised foliage. D. & S., foliage.
2. Foliage. D. & S., foliage.
3. A spray of foliage, finely carved; in the centre, within a quatrefoil, is the bust of a man with pointed beard, holding a scroll. D., the bust of an ecclesiastic, in a trefoil and foliage. S., *broken*.
4. Foliage. D. & S., foliage.

Fig. 1. 5. Foliage. D. & S., foliage.
6. Two birds *counter regardant*, with foliage. D. & S., foliage.

7. An uncouth, badly-carved figure of a man, crowned, seated; his right hand supports the bracket, his left is raised to his head. He wears a jerkin with large square buttons down the front and a belt with a dagger in it, apparently very much in the way. D. & S., stiff conventional foliage. [This seat is fifteenth century work, and forms a striking contrast to the grace of the other examples.]

8. Two arms with attenuated hands and tight sleeves, springing from foliage, assist a trefoil leaf to support the bracket. D. & S., foliage.

9. Two birds standing on leaves, pecking at centre leaf. D. & S., foliage.

10. Foliage. D. & S., foliage.

11. A man supporting the bracket on his shoulders. D. & S., foliage.

12. A merman and mermaid, holding a flat object like a tabor between them; below is a mask. D. & S., maple foliage.

Fig. 3. 13. Foliage. D. & S., foliage.

14. Two fish. D. & S., heads in drapery.

15. A very conventional lion. D. & S., foliage.

16. Foliage. D. & S., foliage.

17. Foliage springing from a demon's head. D. & S., foliage.

18. A double-bodied bird ending in foliage. D. & S., foliage.

19. Fine spray of foliage springing from animal's mouth. D., foliage with demon's head. S., foliage with animal's head.

Fig. 5. 20. A figure with a man's head, crowned, with four legs, hands in front, hoofs behind; the body has a cloth over it, and a saddle with stirrups. It is supposed to represent Nebuchadnezzar in his debasement. D. & S., foliage.

21. A fleur-de-lys. D. & S., foliage.

22. A man kneeling, about to throw a stone with one hand, supporting the bracket with the other. D. & S., foliage.

Fig. 13. 23. An elephant; the earliest known carved example in England, and more true to nature than many later specimens. D. & S., a head.

24. Raised foliage, leaves cross-wise in centre. D. & S., foliage.

Fig. 14. 25. A mermaid, with drapery on her head, holding a fish; her right hand is broken. D. & S., foliage.

26. Foliage. D. & S., foliage.

27. A cock and grotesque. D. & S., foliage.

Fig. 11. 28. Foliage, ending in animal's head in centre. D. & S., foliage.

South Side, commencing West.

1. A lion and dragon fighting. D. & S., a lion's mask; somewhat later in date.

2. Foliage. D. & S., a dragon.

3. Foliage. D. & S., a dragon.

Fig. 9. 4. Two grotesques over a fleur-de-lys. D. & S., foliage.

5. Flat leaves. D. & S., foliage.

Plate 1.

EXETER CATHEDRAL.

Fig. 1.
No. 5, North.

. Fig. 2.
No. 13, South.

Fig. 3.
No. 13, North.

EXETER CATHEDRAL.

Fig. 4.
No 6, South

Fig. 5.
No 20, North

Fig. 6.
No. 7, South.

Plate 3.

Fig. 7.
No. 18, South.

Fig. 8.
Chapter House.

Fig. 9.
No. 4, South.

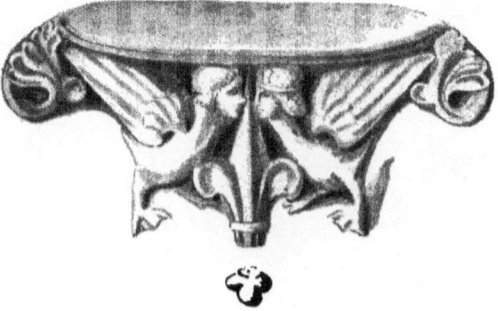

Fig. 10.
No. 15. South.

Fig. 11.
No. 28, North.

Fig. 12.
No. 17, South.

Fig. 13.
No. 23, North

Fig. 14.
No. 25, North

Fig. 15.
No. 16, South

Fig. 4.   6. Two composite animals, with male and female heads, taking hands. D. & S., foliage.

Fig. 6.   7. A human-headed bird, holding a spray. D. & S., foliage.

8. Foliage. D. & S., men in hoods.

9. A female sagittary. D. & S., foliage.

10. A boss of foliage. D. & S., foliage.

11. A knight, with a helmet surmounted by a crown, attacked by a lioness or leopard ; he raises his sword in his right hand (*broken*), and holds a heater-shaped shield in his left ; a very poor defence against such an agile opponent. D., a head in drapery. S., a head in cap, and netted hair at sides.

12. Foliage. D. & S., foliage.

Fig. 2.   13. A knight, kneeling on one knee, thrusting his sword into a grotesque bird, which receives its *coup de grace* with the utmost composure. D. & S., foliage.

14. Foliage. D. & S., foliage.

Fig. 10. 15. A man kneeling, playing a pipe and beating a tabor. D. & S., a dog-like dragon.

Fig. 15. 16. The bracket moulding on each side ends in foliage, which meets in the centre.

Fig. 12. 17. A male sagittary. D. & S., a dog-like dragon, one of which is pierced with the arrow.

Fig. 7.   18. A knight in a boat, towed by a fine swan ; the knight is in chain armour, with surcoat and a late form of the barrel helmet. D. & S., flowers. [This, probably, represents Lohengrin, "the knight of the swan."]

19. Foliage. D. & S., foliage.

20. Foliage. D. & S., foliage.

Fig. 8.   21. Foliage. D. & S., a bird (now in Chapter House).

CHICHESTER CATHEDRAL.

The stalls are forty in number, thirty-eight having misericords. None of them are returned. They are obviously the work of different hands, but they are all fine. The elbows are carved. They date thirteenth century, and were the gift of Bishop Sherborne.

North Side, commencing West.

1. *Missing.*

Fig. 3.   2. A nude man fighting an animal, he thrusts a sword down its throat. D. & S., a winged dragon.

Fig. 15.   3. Two apes. D. & S., a dragon.

4. Foliage. D., a grotesque mask with tongue protruding, upside down. S., the same, but with small arms.

5. Foliage. D. & S., a grotesque dragon.

6. Two hounds seizing a hare between them, and above them is a large bat with extended wings. D. & S., a leaf.

Fig. 6.   7. Two grotesque quadruped scaled monsters standing on their hind legs and supporting the bracket with their fore-claws. D., a demon's head grinning and shewing his teeth. S., a demon's head with tongue protruding.

8. Foliage and fruit. D., a small dragon. S., a hound.

9. A centaur in cape and hood leaning forward, the drapery flowing—his right hand is thrown forward holding some of it—his left is on his flank. D., a head. S., a woman's head.

10. A grotesque dragon in foliage. D. & S., leaf.

11. A crowned head in the centre, large feathered dragons on either side, their tails terminating in heads. D., a grinning mask with tongue protruding. S., a lion's mask with tongue protruding.

12. A large winged dragon. D. & S., leaf.

Fig. 2.   13. A lion's mask with tongue protruding. D. & S., lion's head in profile with tongue protruding.

14. A minstrel in a hood holding a "crowd" or viol in his left hand up to his shoulder. He leans back and kisses a girl posture-maker behind him. Her head is thrown back and her left hand is up in the air. Her right hand is on her girdle. D. & S., face.

Fig. 10. 15. Two dragons, one on either side; a smaller one in the centre. D. & S., leaf.

16. Two large heads, a man, bearded, and a woman, back to back; a dragon below gnaws the woman. D. & S., head.

17. Foliage. D. & S., head.

Plate 6.

Fig. 1.
No. 18, South

Fig. 2.
No. 13, North

Fig. 3.
No. 2, North.

Fig. 4.
No. 9, South.

Fig. 5.
No 5, South.

Fig. 6.
No. 7, North.

Fig. 7.
No. 16, South

Fig. 8.
No. 2, South.

Fig. 9.
No. 15, South.

Fig. 10.
No. 15, North

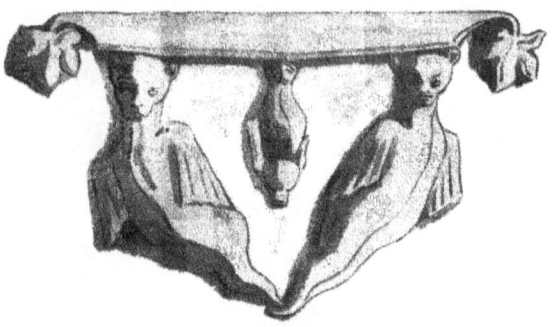

Fig. 11.
No. 11, South

Fig. 12.
No. 17, South

Plate 10.

Fig. 13.
No. 19, South

Fig. 14.
No. 6, South.

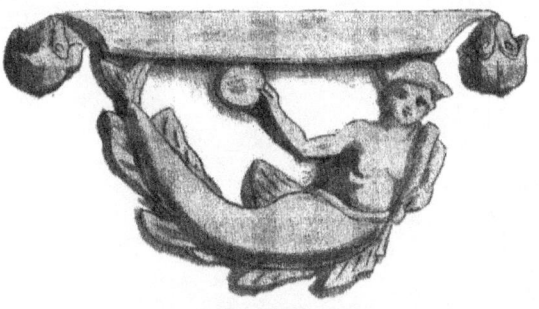

Fig. 15.
No. 3, North

18. A centaur in a hood with very long arms, he holds his tail with his left hand, his right hand is at his side.
19. Foliage. D. & S., leaf.
20. A man, nude but for a hood, dancing with a fiend. D. & S., hooded faces reversed.

South Side, commencing West.

1. *Modern.*

Fig. 8. 2. A dragon. D. & S., hounds' heads reversed.

3. Two large heads in hoods, back to back, the sinister with a carefully curled beard, a hand holding it.

4. Foliage. D., a man's head. S., a woman's head.

Fig. 5. 5. Two men seated in high-backed chairs, the right-hand man playing the harp, the left-hand man the pipe. D., a woman's head in wimple. S., a man's head.

Fig. 14. 6. A mermaid in a cap. In her right hand she holds a mirror; her left hand by her side. She is sad and attenuated. D. & S., hound's head upside down.

7. Two figures intertwined head and tail, one bearded, on the back of a small ass, which is saddled and has its tongue out. D. & S., small dragon.

8. A woman fighting a lion with a sword in her right hand. She thrusts it into the mouth while holding its ear with her left hand. The lion has its left paw on her right knee. The whole composition is in foliage. D., a woman's head in wimple and gorget. S., a woman's head.

Fig. 4. 9. A grotesque human-headed quadruped with curly beard. It has hands to its fore-legs and hoofs behind. D. & S., grotesque face.

10. An ape drowning a dragon. D., a woman's head. S., a man's head.

Fig. 11. 11. A lion-bodied man with clawed hind-legs playing the tabor. He has a cape and hood. D. & S., leaf.

12. Two dragons fighting over a child's head which lies below in the centre, their right and left claws resting on it. D. & S., heads of jesters biting the tails of their hoods.

13. Foliage. D. & S., lion's mask.

14. Foliage. D. & S., oak foliage.

Fig. 9. 15. Two dragons interlaced. D. & S., man's head.

Fig. 7. 16. A bird between two apes who support the bracket with their hands. D. & S., heads in hoods.

Fig. 12. 17. A tapir-like griffin. D. & S., grotesque mask.

Fig. 1. 18. A double-bodied lion seated, its fore-paws meeting in the centre and its tail passing through its legs and over its shoulders. D. & S., dragon.

Fig. 13. 19. A bearded posture-maker contorting himself by pulling his legs with his hands. He wears knee-breeches and thick-soled shoes. D. & S., small dragon.

20. A fox playing the harp to the left. A goose below him listening, and a monkey to the left dancing to the dulcet strains. D. & S., leaf.

E

WINCHESTER CATHEDRAL.

There are sixty-eight stalls in all, sixty-two being in the higher row (ten returned under the screen), and six returned in the lower row. The elbows of each alternate stall have been cut away to allow the later canopied work to be supported by pillars, and old elbows have been fitted on the more modern seats throughout the choir, some being very good; they date about the commencement of the fourteenth century.

[The misericords differ from those in other series, in that the centre groups are small, while the "supporters" are large and more important. Some of the foliage is beautifully carved, but the small size of the illustrations prevents justice being done to it.]

North Side, commencing West.

1. The head of an ecclesiastic in a mitre. D. & S., oak leaves.
2. A man seated in a crouching attitude; his hands, which are large (out of all proportion), are placed on his knees. D. & S., oak leaves and acorns.
3. A human-headed biped monster. The head is that of a woman in wimple and gorget; the mouth is very large. D. & S., birds in foliage.
4. Foliage. D. & S., square foliated ornament.
5. A posture-maker, grimacing. D. & S., leaves.
6. A man squatting down and playing the pipe. D. & S., leaves.
7. A posture-maker turning a somersault (*the head gone*). D., the crowned head of a king. S., a woman's head with curly hair.
8. A human-headed bird. D., a mermaid with her comb in her right hand. S., a merman with a fish in his left hand. *(Fig. 2.)*
9. An owl with out-spread wings. D. & S., beech leaves and nuts. *(Fig. 1.)*
10. A fool-bishop in a cap with long ears (*the right broken off*), clasping a pastoral staff with his hands. D., a man with hood drawn over his head, fighting a wolf or dog which bites his left cheek; he seizes the animal's back with his left hand, and with his right thrusts a sword into its hind-quarters. S., the figure of an old woman, whose hair is confined in a net; in her arms she bears a distaff, the bobbin of which she twirls with her right hand, while she feels the yarn with her left; behind her is a large cat. *(Fig. 3.)*
11. A foliated head. D. & S., foliage.

Fig. 1.
No. 9, North.

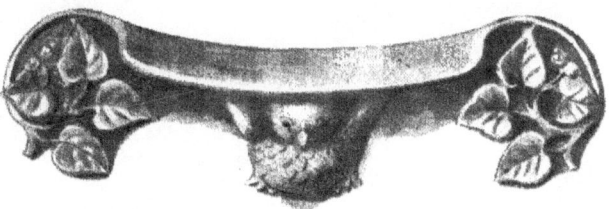

Fig. 2.
No. 8, North.

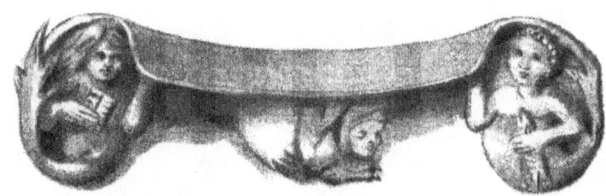

Fig. 3.
No. 10, North.

Plate 12.

Fig. 4.
No. 23, North.

Fig. 5.
No. 19, North.

Fig. 6.
No. 17, North.

Plate 13.

Fig. 7
No. 12, North.

Fig. 8.
No. 26, North.

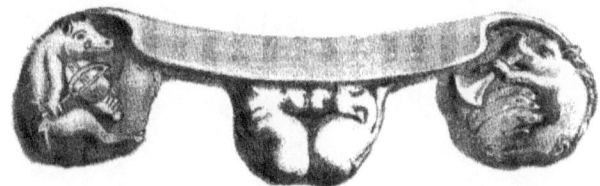

Fig. 9.
No. 32, North.

Fig. 7.　12.　A fool, or posture-maker, lying on his side, and attempting to draw his sword with his right hand; with the left he holds the scabbard. His head lolls on one side, and his tongue protrudes. D., a double-bodied monster, winged. S., two dragons fighting; they have long tails, which are interlaced, and they have both long ears.

13.　A man making a grimace by extending his mouth with his hands. D. & S., foliage.

14.　A lion, the hind legs very long. D., a small naked boy in foliage. S., a monster in foliage.

15.　A grotesque, clothed in quilted leather, his head lolling on one side. D. & S., leaves.

16.　A large cat's head. D. & S., leaves.

Fig. 6.　17.　The figures of two men. One man has an enormous mouth, or wears a mask; their wrists are bound together with a rope. They are apparently a pair of "Davenport Brothers," and will, probably, untie the knots themselves. D. & S., foliage.

18.　A bearded head, with hands on either side.

Fig. 5.　19.　A posture-maker, his legs crossed over his head. D. & S., a foliated mask.

20.　An ape and an owl; the former is bringing the bird forward, and grinning at its blinking in the sunlight.

21.　*Missing.*

22.　A woman in wimple and gorget, seated, her hands resting on her knees. D., a female tumbler in foliage, her head thrown back, and her foot held up by her left hand. S., a male supporter, very similar; his right hand is under his chin, and his left hand holds up his foot.

Fig. 4.　23.　A ram's head with curly horns. D., an ape playing the harp. S., a dog curled up.

24.　A grotesque face. D. & S., foliated mask.

25.　An ape holding up a two-handled pitcher. D. & S., leaves.

Fig. 8.　26.　Two dogs standing on their hind-legs, their muzzles together. D., a boar playing the viol, while another listens. S., a sow playing the double pipe, while supplying her litter with requisite nourishment; a little pig listens enchanted in the background.

27.　A woman's head in wimple and gorget, the gorget drawn over her mouth. D. & S., leaves.

28.　A piece of diaper-work (?). D. & S., foliated ornaments.

29.　A fox running away with a goose in its mouth. D., squirrels in beech trees, eating beech nuts.

30.　A woman's head in wimple and gorget. D., a smaller woman's head in similar dress, the gorget being drawn over the mouth. S., a small head of a man, bearded.

31.　A head of a man in a hood of mail. D. & S., dragon.

Fig. 9.　32.　A man seated, crouching; his hands clasped round his knees. D., foliated mask, with tongue protruding. S., a foliated mask.

South Side, commencing West.

1. A woman's head. D., *missing.* S., ivy leaves.
2. A man supporting the bracket with his hands and shoulders.
3. A dog lying down. D. & S., leaves.
4. A ram with curly horns, lying down. D. & S., leaves.
5. A man's head with curly hair. D., a woman's head, the gorget over her mouth. S., a man's head.
6. A grotesque human-headed monster. D. & S., leaves.
7. A man winding a hunting-horn, a hood drawn over his head. D. & S., leaves.
8. A peasant woman seated crouching, supporting the bracket with her back. D., a woman's head in wimple and gorget. S., a man's head in a hood.
9. A hare or rabbit feeding. D. & S., foliage.
10. A peasant kneeling, his hands bound together. D. & S., foliage.
11. A demon with horns and tail. D., a woman's head in wimple and gorget. S., a woman's head, her veil fastened on her head by a chaplet on which are small escalloped ornaments.
12. A human-headed winged monster. D. & S., leaves.
13. A lion's mask. D. & S., foliated masks.
14. A boar, tusked. D. & S., ivy leaves and berries.
15. A female-headed monster with long serpentine tail. D. & S., leaves.
16. A woman's head in wimple and gorget. D. & S., leaves.
17. A female head with no cap, but a profusion of hair. D. & S., leaves.
18. A fox issuing from its earth. D. & S., cocks.
19. A wolf or dog attacking a prostrate man who in his terror cries out and endeavours to hold back the animal by the ear. The wolf has his paws on the man's throat. D. & S., leaves.
20.
21. *Missing.*
22.
23. A man seated crouching; his head bent forward and the palms of his hands by his cheeks.
Fig. 11. 24. A demi-figure of a man upside down. D. & S., human-headed birds or harpies hooded, in foliage.
Fig. 13. 25. A woman seated sideways to the left. D. & S., a boy with foliage.
26. The demi-figure of a woman upside down. D., woman's head. S., man's head.
Fig. 12. 27. A large head of a man with hood drawn over it. D. & S., foliage.
Fig. 10. 28. A masked figure, or an ape, his arm round the neck of an ape in female dress. D., a woman playing a double pipe. S., woman playing the viol.
29. A human-headed bird or harpy in a hood. D. & S., foliage.
30. A man seated crouching, his hands on his head. D. & S., leaves.
Fig. 14. 31. A fox biting his near hind-foot. D. & S., leaves.

Fig. 10.
No. 28, South.

Fig. 11.
No. 24, South

Fig. 12.
No. 27, South.

Fig. 13.
No. 25, South

Fig. 14.
No. 31, South.

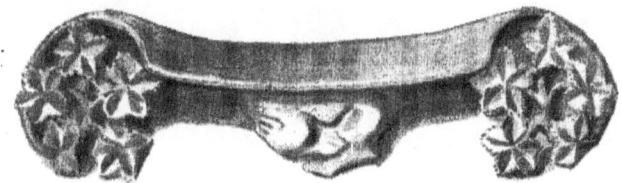

Fig. 15.
No. 2, South.
Lower Row.

Lower Row, North.

1. A peasant laughing, long leather gauntlets on his hands. D., woman's head in wimple and gorget. S., man's head in a hood.
2. A large head with tongue protruding. D. & S., leaves
3. A man's head. D. & S., leaves.

Lower Row, South.

1. A man extending the corners of his mouth with his hands. D. & S., leaves.

Fig. 15. 2. A harpy with large talons. D. & S., leaves.

3. A man in chain armour with a hood. He carries a short broad-sword and a small round target. D. & S., human-headed bird.

ALL SAINTS' CHURCH, SUTTON COURTENEY, BERKSHIRE.

The church of this picturesque village possesses three misericords of the thirteenth century, but they are rather broken, and are not in their original position.

Fig. 1.   1. A boss, apparently representing a lion fighting a dragon, or perhaps devouring his prey. D. & S., conventional ornament.

Fig. 2.   2. A wide-mouthed lion. D. & S., small ball flower.

Fig. 3.   3. A falcon striking a bird. D. & S., small ornament.

Plate 16.

Fig. 1.

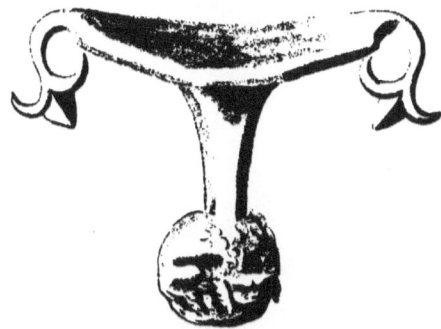

Fig. 2.

Fig. 3.

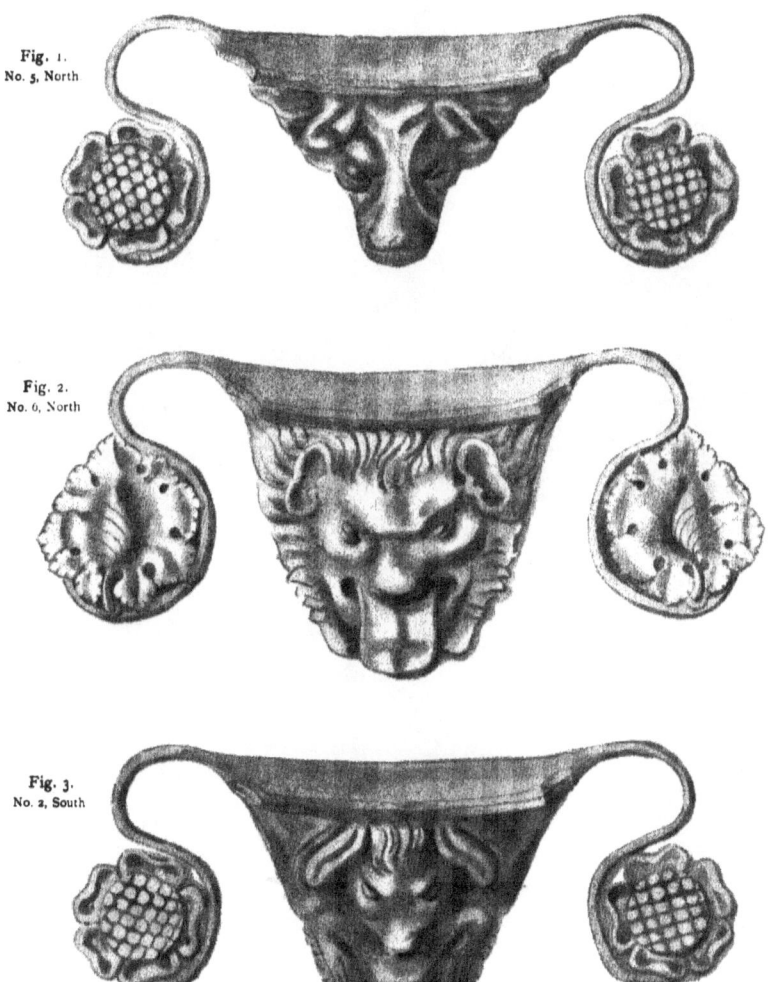

Fig. 1.
No. 5, North

Fig. 2.
No. 6, North

Fig. 3.
No. 2, South

FORDHAM, CAMBRIDGESHIRE.

The church was given by Henry III. to the great Gilbertine Monastery at Sempringham. There are twelve stalls in the chancel. The elbows are carved with demi-angels and lions. They apparently date the early part of the fourteenth century.

North Side, commencing West.

1. Foliage. D. & S., foliage.
2. A grotesque human-headed monster, winged, with webbed feet. D. & S., foliage.
3. The head of a bull. D. & S., a single rose.
4. A similar monster to No. 2, but with a lion's face. D. & S., sunflowers.
Fig. 1. 5. A bull's face. D. & S., a single rose.
Fig. 2. 6. A lion's head with tongue protruding. D. & S., a vine leaf.

South Side, commencing West.

1. A shield, uncharged. D. & S., foliage.
Fig. 3. 2. A grotesque monster, winged, and with webbed feet. D. & S., a single rose.
3. A lion's mask. D. & S., sunflowers.
4. Lion's mask with tongue protruding. D. & S., foliage.
5. A shield, charged : a fess and six fusils. D. & S., a leaf.
6. A flower. D. & S., foliage.

ELY CATHEDRAL.

The stalls were erected by Alan de Walsingham, Bishop 1332. The work was commenced in 1338, according to the Lambeth copy of the Chronicle (*Lambeth MSS.*, 448); and in the Sacrist's Roll of 13 Edward III., there is a notice of payment of 13s. 4d. on account of it: "*Soluti ad fabricam Stallorum hoc anno pro O et olla sacrista.*"

The misericords are set very near the ground; the carving of the seats is excellent, but the position in which they are fixed is most awkward for seeing it. The brackets are of unusual width, and slope downward, so that the heavy shadow thrown on the work makes it, in some cases, next to impossible to make out the subject.

North Side, commencing West:, Upper Row.

1. Two demi-angels, supporting a shield bearing a fess *dancette*; below are two birds. D & S., leaves (*modern*).
2. Two grotesque faces in foliage. D. & S., leaves.
3. A stag. D., a huntsman winding his horn; he is accompanied by his hounds; he carries his bow on his right shoulder, and his arrows are suspended in a quiver. S., a stag.
4. A man in a long cloak, leaning forward and clasping his knees. D. & S., leaves.
5. A man with two hounds in leash, a hare slung over his back. D., a boy with a hound. S., a hare running into foliage.
6. Two lions issuing from foliage. D. & S., vine leaves and foliage.
7. A man bending forward, his hands resting on his knees; the bracket is supported on his shoulders. D. & S., foliage.
8. A woman, seated; a tree growing up beneath her feet, and with two branches springing from it like the letter Y. Through the fork peers her face, her arms are raised, and support the bracket. D. & S., stags browsing.
9. A man clad in a long tunic, leaning forward, and resting his hands on his knees; he is bearded. D. & S., lions biting themselves.
10. A man in a vine, gathering grapes. D. & S., vine leaves and grapes.
11. A woman kneeling; her hands clasped, praying (or, perhaps, confessing) to a seated man. D., a skull wreathed in foliage. S., foliage.
12. A pelican *in her piety*. D. & S., flowers and foliage.
13. A man leaning on his sword, which is held in his left hand. D. & S., oak foliage.
14. A face in oak foliage. D. & S., oak foliage.

Fig. 1.

Fig. 1.
No. 5, North

Fig. 2.
No. 16, North

Fig 3.
No. 18, South.
Lower Row.

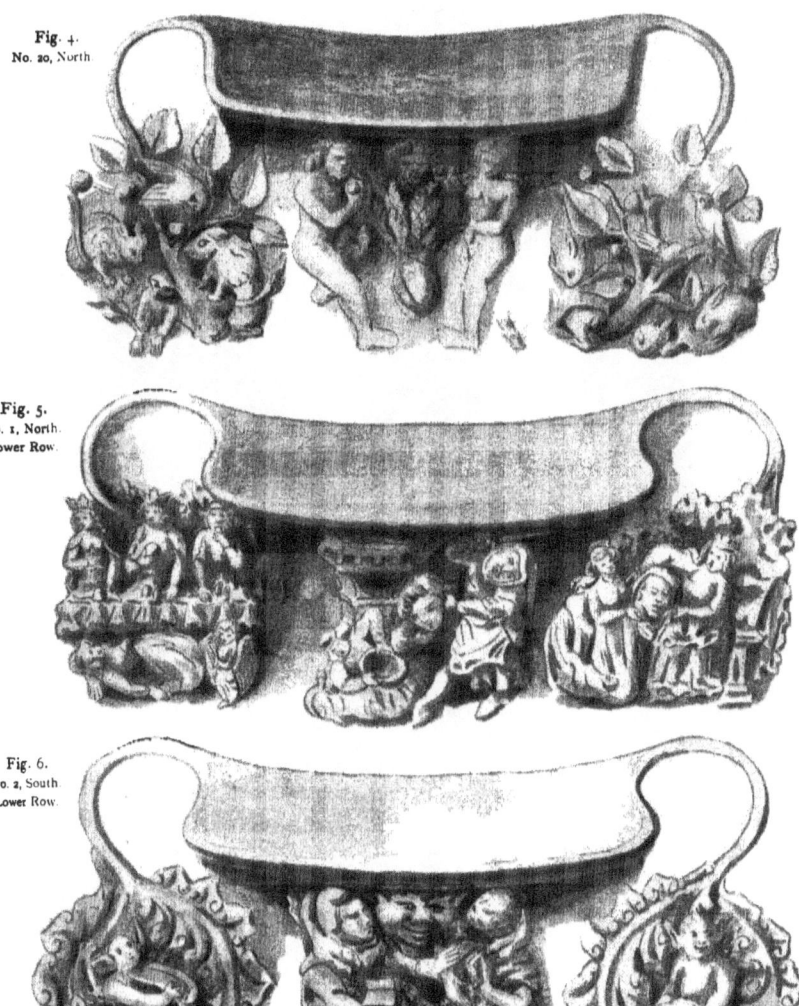

ELY CATHEDRAL.

Plate 19.

Fig. 4.
No. 20, North

Fig. 5.
No. 1, North.
Lower Row.

Fig. 6.
No. 2, South.
Lower Row.

Fig. 7. 15. Two wrestlers or tumblers, head and tail (or boys playing "all fours"). The upper figure wears a cap with ears to it. D. & S., lion and griffin fighting.

Fig. 2. 16. A man and horse falling to the ground; the man wears a tight-fitting cap and a loose jerkin. His hunting-horn lies broken beside him. D., two dogs hunting hinds through a wood. S., a woman (or saint) in a chapel praying before a small altar. [This may refer to the legend of St. Giles, Seat 18, South.]

17. A woman with a small unicorn in her arms. D., a man with helmet on head, the vizor down, armed with a shield, sword, and battle-axe. S., A man with sword and spear, or staff, in a wood.

18. Two women seated, side by side, their hands on their knees. D. & S., flowers.

19. A fox running away with a fat goose, but not undisturbed, as the good-wife belabours him with her distaff. D., a fox in a monk's cowl, with a pastoral staff in his hand, preaching to a cock and two hens. S., a man with a flail standing before a crop of wheat.

Fig. 4. 20. The Temptation in the Garden. The "tree of knowledge" stands in the centre, round which is entwined the serpent with human head. Adam is about to eat one apple, and holds another in his hand; Eve looks on. D., an ape, and two jerboa-like animals in foliage. S., a rabbit-warren, with birds in foliage.

21. A woman seated, her hands on her knees. D. & S., leaves.

22. A man leaning forward (*broken*). D. & S., oak leaves and acorns.

23. Two men, bearded, their hoods over their heads, seated at a table playing dice. D., a woman, seated on a bench, holding a spray of flowers; beside her, a beer-barrel. S., a man in a long tunic, carrying a cup in one hand and a bottle in the other.

Fig. 10. 24. A man kneeling on one knee, and supporting the bracket with his hands. D., a man playing the "crowd" or viol. S., a dog lying curled up.

South Side, commencing West: Upper Row.

1. Two demi-angels supporting a shield, uncharged. D. & S., oak leaves (*modern*).

2. Two jesters, seated on a bench, their heads on one side; their inner hands rest on their knees. The elbows of the outer arms rest on the bench. D., a lion's mask, from which issues foliage. S., birds in foliage.

3. Noah looking out of the Ark, which is represented as a three-towered castle, on a clinker-built boat. D., a raven perched on the carcase of an ox. S., the dove, flying towards Noah, with the olive branch. Water runs along, below all the subjects, on the misericord.

4. A woman seated, leaning forward, her hands raised on each side of her face, but not touching it. D. & S., lions in oak foliage.

Fig. 11. 5. A long-handed ape stooping down, with drapery over its shoulders. D. & S., winged dragon; its tail a prolongation of the bracket moulding.

6. A woman seated in a chair, her hands resting on the heads of two hounds which stand one on each side of her. D. & S., apes in foliage.

F

7. A man grimacing, his hands resting on his knees and his legs turned up behind him. D. & S., oak leaves.

Fig. 9. 8. A man with his arms round two monsters with serpents' bodies. D., a centaur playing pipe and tabor. S., a female centaur playing the dulcimer. Both in foliage.

9. A man seated, his legs crossed and his hands on his knees; he has long hair and a beard. D. & S., oak leaves.

10. A man and woman seated; he crosses his right foot on to his left knee. D. & S., oak leaves.

11. A man seated, his arms extended and supporting the bracket. D. & S., foliage.

12. A man squatting down, his head supporting the bracket, his arms under his chin. D. & S., lions biting themselves.

Fig. 8. 13. Two crowned figures seated, in voluminous and carefully-carved drapery. D. & S., three birds with their heads to the centre.

14. A king, crowned, seated on a throne under arcading; his arms crossed in front of him. D. & S., two figures [? angels] kneeling in adoration towards the centre figure.

15. A figure in jester's cap (*the body gone*), standing in the water. D., a child riding on a dog, which looks back. S., a dog or lion taking a child out of the water in its mouth.

16. Samson astride the lion, whose jaws he is tearing open. D. & S., foliage.   .

17. A woman nursing a child whose arms are round her neck. D. & S., foliage.

18. A fiend opening a man's mouth, and endeavouring to pull out a tooth; he seizes the man's beard in so doing. D. & S., foliage.

19. A man squatting down; one arm is behind his head and the other supports it. D. & S., apes in foliage.

20. A bear below a tree, in which are two apes. D. & S., apes in foliage.

21. A monk and nun in a situation concerning which the less said the better.

22. A man seated, leaning forward; his hands behind him. D. & S., foliage.

23. Two men seated, their heads resting on their hands. D. & S., foliage.

North Side, commencing West: Lower Row.

Fig. 5. 1. The story of the death of St. John the Baptist, in three compartments. The daughter of Herodias receiving the head of the saint from the gaoler; the prison in the background. D., a table, at which are seated Herod, Philip and Herodias; in front of the table the daughter dances, or rather tumbles (*Saltavit*). S., the mother receiving the head in a charger from the daughter. The mother is crowned.

2. An owl perched in a tree, holding a mouse under its left claw. D. & S., foliage, in which are small birds.

3. A man fallen down under trees; he holds a billet of wood in each hand. D., a man blowing his horn in a boar hunt. S., two men armed with swords and bucklers.

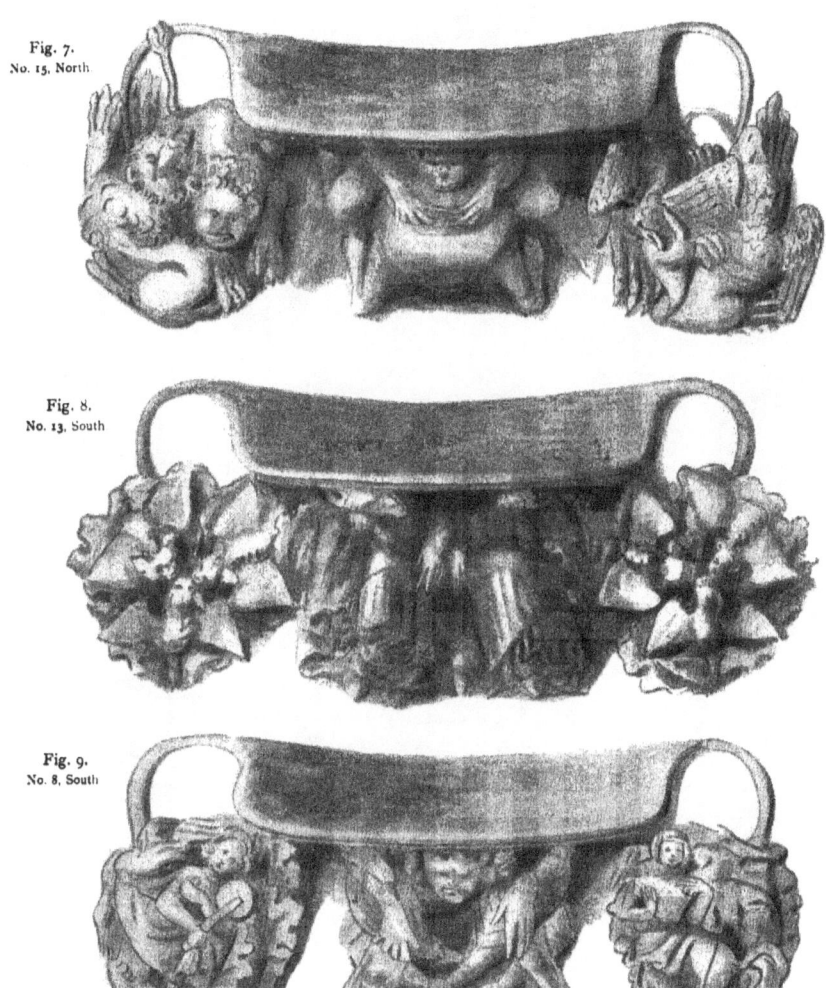

Fig. 7.
No. 15, North

Fig. 8.
No. 13, South

Fig. 9.
No. 8, South

ELY CATHEDRAL.

ELY CATHEDRAL.

Plate 21.

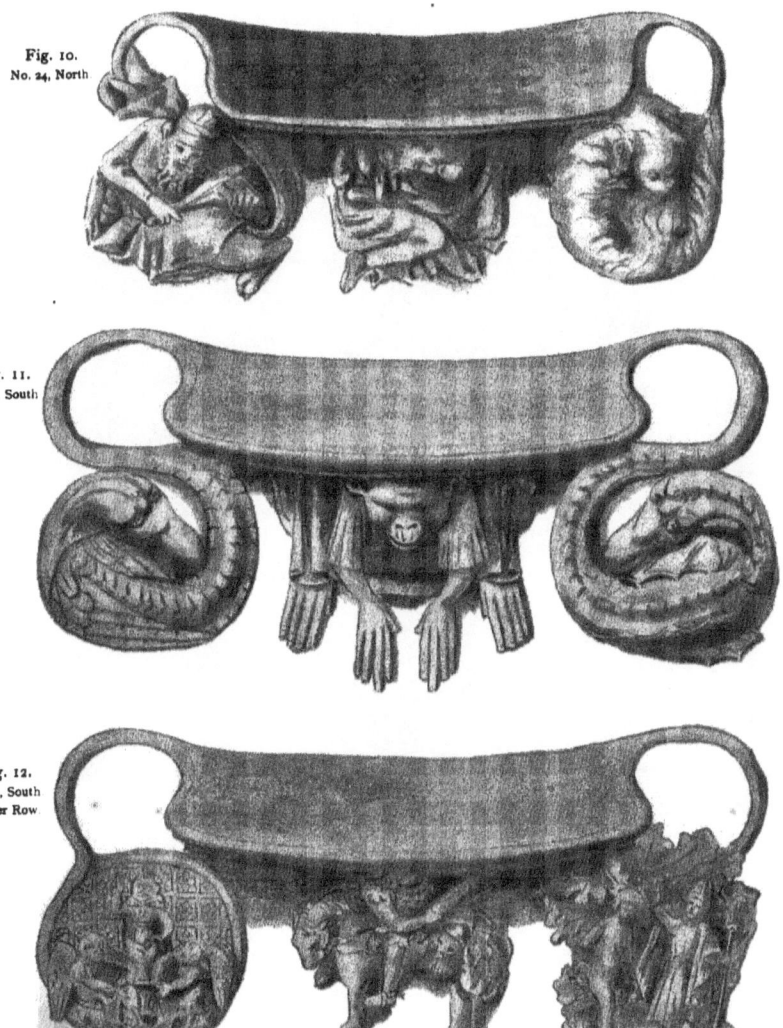

Fig. 10.
No. 24, North

Fig. 11.
No. 5, South

Fig. 12.
No. 1, South
Lower Row

4. A king, crowned, stooping down, resting his head on his right hand; his left grasps the skirt of his mantle. D. & S., leaves and grapes.

5. The expulsion from Eden. Adam and Eve being driven out by the angel, who bears a large sword. D., a man and boy, the latter stooping. S., a woman with a distaff, a cat playing with the yarn.

6. A man seated, his hands on his knees (*Modern*). D. & S., leaves.

7. A man kneeling on the ground, supporting the bracket with one hand (*Modern*).

8. A man seated on the ground, playing the "crowd." D. & S., oak leaves and acorns. (*Modern*).

9. A bearded man, seated on the ground, holding a scroll in front of him. D. & S., dragons in foliage.

10. A woman seated, supporting the bracket with her hands. D. & S., roses and leaves (*Modern*).

11. A woman seated, with a unicorn in her lap. D. & S., leaves (*Modern*).

12. A man kneeling, his head supporting the bracket. D. & S., leaves (*Modern*).

13. The emblem of St. Luke, a bull and book. D. & S., leaves (*Modern*.)

14. St. Matthew with book before him, which is supported by an angel. D. & S., leaves (*Modern*),

15. St. John the Evangelist with eagle, in his hand the poisoned cup. (*Modern*.)

16. A man seated on the ground, a book in his right hand, a pilgrim's staff in his left. D. & S., leaves (*Modern*).

17. Two women grinding corn. They are surrounded by cooking utensils. D. & S., leaves.

18. A bishop in a mitre, with a pilgrim's staff. (*Modern*).

19. St. Peter kneeling, with books and keys. D. & S., sheaves and fruit (*Modern*).

South Side, commencing West : Lower Row.

Fig. 12. 1. A knight, armed *cap-à-pie*, riding, and aiming a blow at a figure, all head and no body, behind him. D., a figure of Our Lord in the act of benediction (*his head and orb gone*), two angels adoring, one on either side, swing censers; the background is diapered. S., a bishop in mitre, exorcising a spirit out of a nude figure; the spirit is of female form.

[It has been suggested that the centre subject is intended for St. Martin dividing his cloak with the beggar; the figure behind the knight has a crutch. The hind-leg of the knight's horse is broken off close to the body, which makes an awkward gap, and gives the figure behind an uncouth appearance.]

Fig. 6. 2. Two women at their devotions, between whom the devil pokes his head, and puts his arms round their necks. The woman to the left has a chaplet round her head and carries a rosary; the other holds a book. D. & S., small fiends with scrolls, in foliage.

3. A man and woman riding on a horse; she holds its tail, which is pulled over its back; he grasps its mane. It has knocked down two people, over whom they are riding. D. & S., four persons, two men and two women, looking on in astonishment.

4. Two men clothed in long loose tunics, wrestling, their hands clasped. D. & S., leaves.

5. A ram under two oak trees. D. & S., leaves.

6. A woman seated, holding a book. D. & S., oak leaves and acorns (*Modern*).

7. A hooded figure, seated under an oak tree. D. & S., ivy leaves (*Modern*).

8. A man seated, his hands on his knees. D. & S., leaves (*Modern*).

9. An old man kneeling, wearing a loose cap, supporting the bracket with his left hand. D. & S., leaves.

10. A man kneeling on one knee, supporting the bracket with his head and one hand. D. & S., leaves (*Modern*).

11. A bearded man squatting down, his head on one side. D. & S., ivy leaves and fruit.

12. A man seated under an arcading. D. & S., ivy leaves (*Modern*).

13. A bearded man, his hood drawn over his head, seated, bending forward. D. & S., ivy leaves.

14. A knight, fully armed, kneeling on one knee, his body supporting the bracket; he has a vizor to his helmet, and carries a sword and battle-axe. D. & S., leaves.

15. A man seated. D. & S., leaves.

16. A man and woman seated on the ground, fighting; he has his right thumb in the woman's mouth, while she strikes him in the face, and kicks his knee. D. & S., grotesque lions with foliated tails.

17. A man kneeling on one knee, supporting the bracket; he holds one hand behind his head, and the other on his hip. D., two rams fighting, foliage behind. S., an eagle carrying off a lamb.

Fig 3. 18. A bearded man in a cave or cell, stooping down and caressing a hind; he carries a rosary in his other hand. D. & S., archers in foliage, shooting at the hind. This is, no doubt, the legend of St. Giles [*see Subject List*]. In the drawing, the arrow seems to be in the body of the hind, whereas it should be in the saint's knee.

Fig. 1.
No 4, South.

Fig. 2.
No. 3, North

Fig. 3.
No 3, South.

ST. ANDREW'S CHURCH, SOHAM, CAMBRIDGESHIRE.

There are ten misericords in the chancel. The seats are of a peculiar shape, without "supporters." The elbows are all carved with a small bunch of foliage. Date, fifteenth century. The church belonged in 1285 to the Cistercian monastery at Rewley, near Oxford, and in 1450 it became the property of Pembroke College, Cambridge.

North Side, commencing West.

	1.	The head of a fool or jester in a cap with long ears.
Fig. 4.	2.	A man's face, the tongue protruding.
Fig. 2.	3.	A woman's head with wimple and gorget.
	4.	} *Broken.*
	5.	

South Side, commencing West.

Fig. 6.	1.	A monk's head in a circle.
Fig. 5.	2.	A woman's face, laughing, her hair in a net.
Fig. 3.	3.	A man's head, three-quarter face.
Fig. 1.	4.	A woman's head.
	5.	A man's head, bearded.

ST. KATHARINE BY THE TOWER.

The Hospital and Collegiate church of St. Katharine, standing
within the precincts of the Tower, were founded and established by
Matilda, Queen-Consort of King Stephen, in 1148. The charity was
suppressed and re-founded on the same site by Eleanor, Queen-Dowager
of Henry III., in 1273. In 1825 they were both swept away to make
room for the great commercial docks, "to which the name of the
patroness of the hospital, St. Katharine, has been strangely applied."
Fragments of the glass and woodwork have been preserved in the
modern hospital in the Regent's Park. There were twenty-four stalls
in the old chapel, eight being returned. Of these only eleven have
survived the vandalism mentioned, five being at the west end of the
chapel, and six being in the so-called chapter-house. They were begun
by William de Enderby, Master in 1340, and completed by John de
Hemensthorpe in 1369. Queen Philippa, wife to Edward III., was
a great patroness to the church.

At the time of the removal some of the seats were given by
the Regent to a friend of his, together with a house in the park, just
opposite. These appear to have been removed during a sale of
furniture by a later tenant ; some of the old glass still remains in the
dining room, but even this is threatened with destruction by the
present owner, because it does not go well with the wall-paper !

In the Chapel, commencing South.

1. A dragon. D. & S., a leaf.

Fig. 3. 2. A bearded man in profile, his head bound with a kerchief, probably a portrait. D.
& S., a grotesque human-headed monster with two claws and winged. They bite
the ends of the bracket moulding.

Fig. 1. 3. A lion devouring a dragon. D. & S., dragon curled up in a circle, one ribbed
transversely, the other longitudinally.

Fig. 1.
No. 3, Chapel

Fig. 2.
No. 4, Chapel.

Fig. 3.
No. 2, Chapel

.

Fig. 4.
No. 3, Chapter House

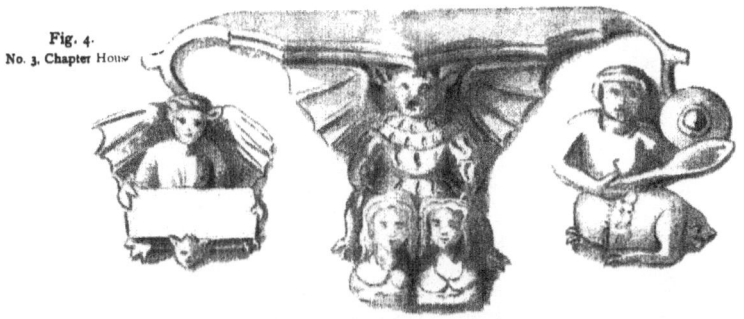

Fig. 5.
No. 5, Chapel.

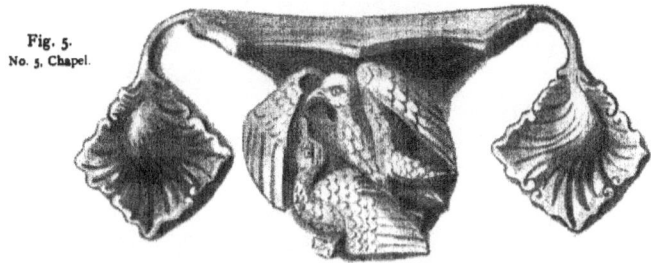

Fig. 6.
No. 4, Chapter House

Fig. 2. 4. An elephant, on whose back is bound a crenellated tower, whence issues a large head of a young woman with a jewelled band round the forehead. The elephant is surrounded by foliage, which no doubt represents a forest. The legend may refer to some imprisoned princess. D., a human-headed biped monster, bearded. S., a human-headed biped monster, clean shaven and cloaked.

Fig. 5. 5. A falcon with its talons fastened in the back of a mallard. D. & S., a leaf.

In the Chapter House, commencing by the Door.

1. A foliated head. D. & S., square foliated ornament.
2. A pelican *in her piety.* D. & S., swan, *gorged, naiant.*
Fig. 4. 3. The demi-figures of two women seated, behind whom sits a fiend. D., a grinning fiend holding the scroll of infamy. S., a fiend with a steel cap or morison on his head ; in his left hand he holds a round target and in his right a club.
Fig. 6. 4. A demi-angel with extended wings, playing the bagpipe, ending in folded drapery, to indicate flying. D., a lion's mask with tongue protruding. S., a lion's mask.
5. A bearded head. D. & S., a rose.
6. Foliage. D. & S., a leaf.

Besides the above there are illustrations of six more given in Ducarel, *Bibl. Top. Brit.*, Vol. II.

A. A monstrous bird or dragon with extended wings. D., a grotesque semi-human monster, a round cap on its head ; its tongue protrudes. It is armed with a round target and a bill. S., a mermaid armed with dagger and shield (?).
B. A harpy or cockatrice. D. & S., leaves.
C. An imp, winged, with protruding ribs, beating two drums which rest on its knees. D., an imp, winged, riding on a rabbit and playing some musical instrument. S., an imp riding a hound side-saddle, and holding on to the animal's tail ; in its other hand it holds a trumpet which it plays with both nose and mouth.
D. A large head of an old woman, veiled, in a wimple ; a gorget round the lower part of her face. D. & S., leaves.
E. A woman clad in a loose robe, riding a human-headed scaly monster, to whose hair she clings with her left hand. D. & S., lion's heads with tongues protruding.
F. A figure, seated, the head gone, with a book in the left hand ; a small figure behind. D., a head wrapped in a hood. S., a human-headed biped monster.

LINCOLN CATHEDRAL.

The fine stalls in this cathedral number one hundred and eight altogether. They are placed in two rows, sixty-two in the upper row, with twelve returned, and forty-two in the lower row, with eight returned. The elbows are finely carved. The stall work is due to the Treasurer, John de Welbourne. "*Inceptor et consultor inceptionis fueture stallorum nivorum in Cathedrale ecclesie Lincolniensi.*" As this John de Welbourne died in 1380, the stalls must be put down to the middle or end of the fourteenth century.

North Side, commencing West: Upper Row.

1. A knight in full armour, fighting seven dragons. D. & S., lion's heads, with tongue protruding.
2. A man's head with curly hair. D. & S., rose.
3. A wyvern. D. & S., a wyvern.
4. Foliage. D. & S., foliage.
5. A "wodehouse," or wild man, in an oak forest beating down acorns. D. & S., swine feeding on the acorns.
6. A lion sleeping amid foliage. D. & S., lion sleeping.
7. The head of a woman, crowned. D. & S., leaves.

Fig. 1. 8. An embattled tower with four turrets, between the two innermost a gateway, with a portcullis, the latter about to fall on the hind-quarters of a horse which is passing through. D. & S., heads of watchmen with pointed helmets and camail.
9. Oak foliage. D. & S., wyvern.

Fig. 6. 10. A grotesque head with claws beneath, holding a scroll. D. & S., wyvern *sejant*.
11. Foliage. D. & S., foliage.
12. A boy riding astride a crane, with two cranes pecking at his eyes. D., a crane in a field, pecking corn out of a sack. S., a boy placing a stone in a sling with his left hand. The sling is very carefully carved, the details perfect. On his left stands a sack, and on his right a pot or cauldron with a handle and three legs. A dead crane lies in foliage.
13. Vine foliage. D. & S., vine leaves and grapes.
14. A king's head, crowned. D. & S., the heads of kerns or chiefs looking at him.
15. A square foliated ornament. D. & S., a square foliated ornament.

Plate 25.

Fig. 1.
No. 8, North.

Fig. 2.
No. 28, North.

Fig. 3.
No. 1, North
Lower Row

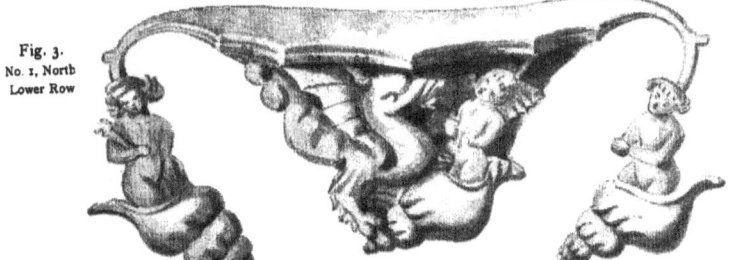

Fig. 4.
No. 24. South.

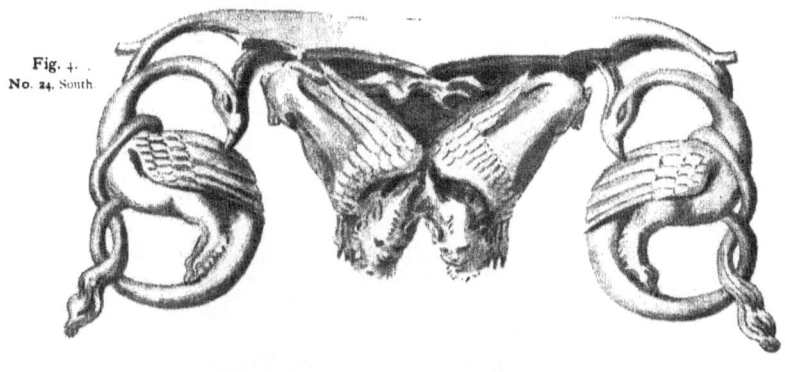

Fig. 5.
No. 20, North

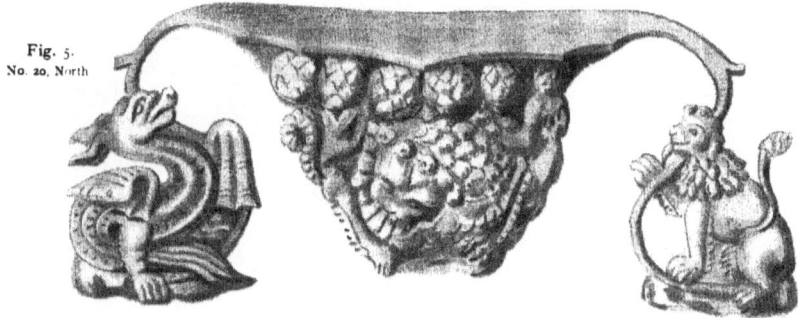

Fig. 6.
No. 10, North

16. The attempted martyrdom of St. John the Evangelist at the Lateran Gate. A cauldron in the centre over a lighted fire; in the cauldron a figure (*broken off at the waist*). On either side of the fire is a man, that on the left blowing up the fire with a pair of bellows. They wear tight jerkins buttoned down the front with large buttons. D. & S., wyvern.

17. A lion seated, his tongue protruding; at his feet are a duck and two ducklings. D. & S., oak leaves.

Fig. 8.   18. A mermaid in the sea, holding a comb in her right and a glass in her left hand. D. & S., lion seated.

19. Oak foliage. D. & S., oak foliage.

Fig. 5.   20. A lion killing a dragon by biting its neck. D., a dragon. S., a lion.

21. A griffin. D. & S., birds in oak foliage.

22. Two men ploughing. The team consists of two oxen with a pair of horses for leaders. D., harrowing. S., sowing.

23. A lion's head with tongue protruding, and claws. D. & S., oak leaves.

24. A human-faced bull with oak leaves. D., a lion-headed monster. S., a human-headed monster with cloven feet.

25. Foliage. D. & S., leaves.

26. A grotesque face amid oak leaves; he has four acorns in his mouth, two on either side. D. & S., oak leaves.

27. Two roses. D. & S., roses.

Fig. 2.   28. A dragon, looking back. D. & S., leaves.

29. Foliage. D. & S., foliage.

30. The Assumption of the Blessed Virgin amid angels. D. & S., angels bearing scrolls circumscribed.

31. The Ascension of our Lord into the clouds; only his feet appear. Below are four Apostles gazing upwards; they are tonsured. D. & S., angels swinging censers.

South Side, commencing West: Upper Row.

1. The Resurrection. Christ stepping from the tomb with an angel on either side. Soldiers in full armour lie asleep below. D., St. Mary Magdalen holding the box of ointment. S., the gardener holding a spade.

Fig. 10.   2. A knight fully armed, his horse falling. D. & S., dragon.

3. A wodehouse and a lion, *passant gardant*. D. & S., foliage.

4. The Coronation of the Virgin. Christ and his mother are under a canopy. Their heads and arms are gone, but the action appears to be that he places a crown on her head. D., an angel with a harp. S., an angel with a lute.

5. A young woman holding a unicorn by its horn. Behind the animal stands a man in full armour (*the upper part of his body broken off.*) D., a human-bodied monster with goat's legs, playing the harp (*the head gone.*) S., a human-bodied lion armed with a shield and knife or falchion; on the shield is a human face.

G

6. A knight and a lady, holding between them a large human mask; a dog lies at their feet. D., a man with a sword under his arm. S., a woman with a wimple over her head, holding a dog in her hands.

7. A king seated cross-legged on a throne. He wears a collar round his neck, his cape is escalloped, and his sword belt is richly jewelled; a sceptre is in his right hand, and a griffin supports him on either side. D. & S., fleur-de-lys.

8. The bust of a king, crowned; he wears a collar of fleurs-de-lys. D. & S., bearded masks with bands round their heads with rose ornaments.

9. The Adoration of the Magi. The Virgin (*much broken*) seated to the right with the Holy Babe in her arms, St. Joseph in a peaked cap behind. The three kings offer homage, one prostrates himself and holds his crown in his left hand. Below are an ox and an ass lying down. D., an angel playing the organ (*broken*). S., an angel *(the arms broken off)*.

10. A wodehouse fighting a griffin. D. & S., wodehouse, seated?

11. A young woman in a long loose robe, holding a bearded man by the hair with her left hand, he cowers down, her right arm is raised to strike him *(hand broken off)*. D. & S., leaves.

12. A lion in an oak tree, beneath is a wyvern. D. & S., oak foliage.

13. A vine with grapes. D. & S., vine leaves.

Fig. 12. 14. A knight in armour lying on the ground, while a lady holds his horse; she is seated and the knight's head rests on her lap. D., a tilting helm, mantled, with a griffin's head as crest; below is a shield, uncharged. S., a man, hooded, issuing from foliage, drawing his sword.

15. A lion's head and paw with foliage. D. & S., foliage.

16. Two apes riding, one a unicorn (*the horn gone*), the other a lion. They wear baldrics, and carry maces and horns. D. & S., hound seated, foliage behind.

Fig. 7. 17. Two birds with fruit. D. & S., two birds drinking from a fountain, one on either side.

Fig. 9. 18. Two dog-like animals D. & S., grotesque with cock's head, animal's body, hoofs and tufted tail.

19. Three roses. D. & S., roses.

20. A wodehouse riding a chained lion, the chain ends in a flower. D. & S., foliage.

21. Oak foliage. D. & S., oak foliage.

22. Two lions, *counter regardant*. D. & S. (*broken*).

23. Human-headed bird, crowned, with out-spread wings. D. & S., leaves.

Fig. 4. 24. Two grotesques. D. & S., a compound animal.

25. A head with thorn foliage. D. & S., square foliated ornaments.

26. A king, crowned, holding a sceptre in his right hand, seated under a canopy; a large square brooch fastens his cloak in front. D., a figure with a book grasping a bough with the right hand. S., a figure amid thorn foliage holding a branch with the right hand.

27. An eagle perched on a globe. D. & S., two leaves.

28. A lion and wyvern fighting. D. & S., human-headed lion.

Fig. 7.
No. 17, South

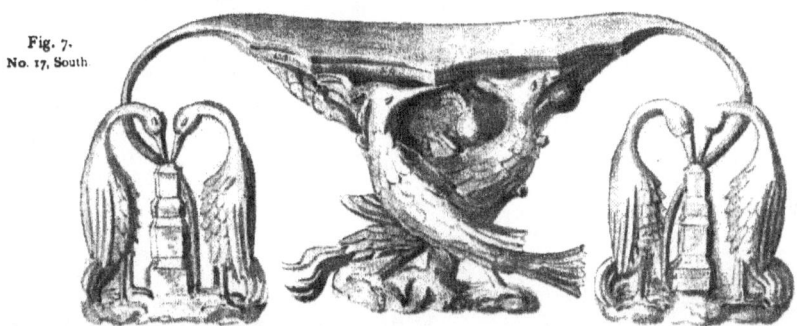

Fig. 8.
No. 18, North.

Fig. 9.
No. 18, South

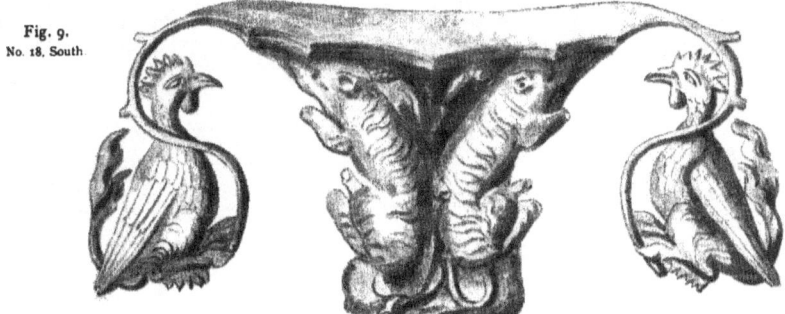

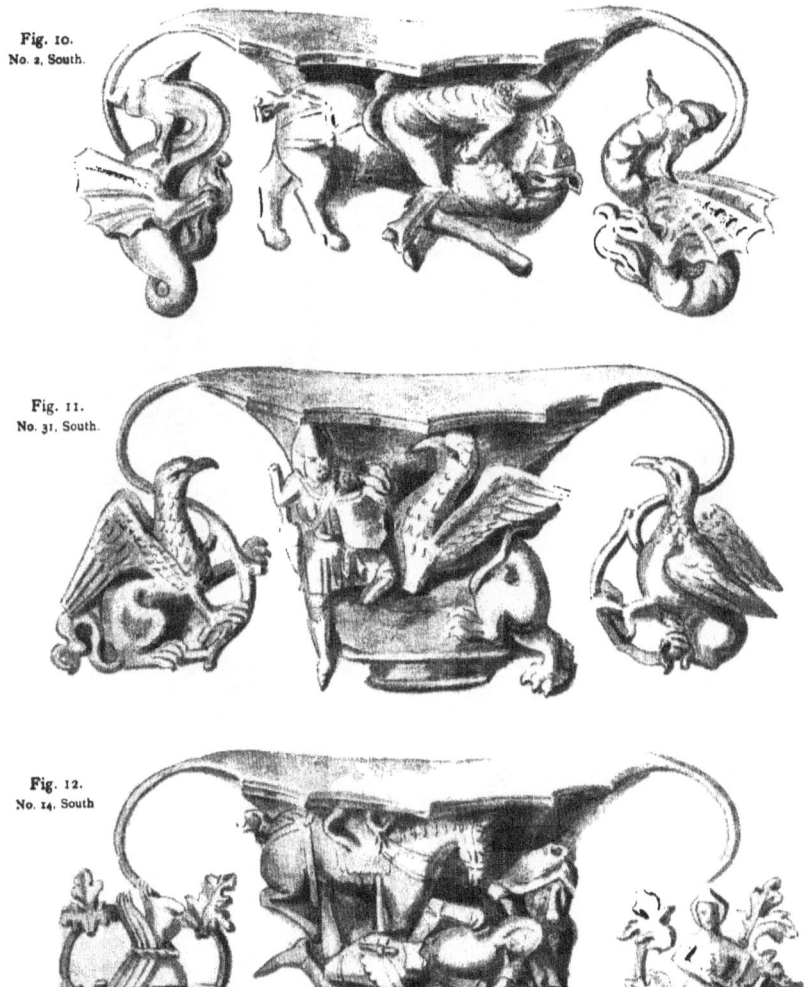

Fig. 10.
No. 2, South.

Fig. 11.
No. 31, South.

Fig. 12.
No. 14, South

29. A wodehouse fighting a lion. D. & S., lion mask with tongue protruding.
30. A human-headed lion bearing a lance with a pennon, and a shield on which is a grotesque head. D. & S., wyvern.

Fig. 11. 31. A knight in armour fighting a griffin. D. & S., griffin. [See No. 14, S.]

North Side, commencing West: Lower Row.

Fig. 3. 1. A winged child, issuing from a spiral shell, fighting with a dragon, which he pierces with a spear. D. & S., child, issuing from spiral shell, with trident.
2. Two apes carrying the corpse of a third on a stretcher; behind, in the centre, is an archway.
3. *Missing.* D. & S., a rose.
4. A lion, sleeping on his back, in a wood. D. & S., foliage.
5. Two dragons fighting. D. & S., foliage.
6. A lion's mask in oak foliage.
7. A pelican *in her piety.* D. & S., smaller pelican.
8. Five roses. D. & S., two roses.
9. A vine issuing from a spiral shell. D. & S., vine leaves.
10. Foliage. D. & S., foliage.
11. ⎫
12. ⎪
13. ⎪
14. ⎬ *Modern.*
15. ⎪
16. ⎪
17. ⎪
18. ⎭
19. A square boss of foliage. D. & S., foliage.
20. Foliage. D. & S., foliage.
21. A lion with two bodies. D. & S., oak leaves.

South Side, commencing West: Lower Row.

1. A demi-angel, bearing a crown. D. & S., faces in foliage.
2. A wyvern. D. & S., wyvern.
3. A niche. D. & S., smaller niche.
4. Foliage. D. & S., foliage.
5. A centaur with sword and shield; the fore-feet are cloven, claws behind.
6. A human-headed monster, with hood drawn over his head. D. & S., square foliated ornament.
7. Two wyverns fighting. D. & S., wyvern.

8. A man seated on a lion, pulling its jaws open; he wears a hood with long ears. D. & S., lion.

9. A human-headed monster, with webbed feet, a dragon's body, and lion's tail. D. & S., small lion with tongue protruding.

10. A dragon and lion in oak foliage. D. & S., dragon and foliage.

11. An eagle and a dragon. D. & S., small eagle.

12. Two dragons, their necks intertwined, fighting. D. & S., dragon, seated.

13. A knight in full armour, mounted on a horse, spearing a dragon. D. & S., lion.

The remainder are modern.

Fig. 1.

Fig. 2.

Fig. 3.

ROTHWELL CHURCH, NORTHAMPTONSHIRE.

There were originally eight seats with misericords, but one has vanished. They date late fifteenth century. A large number of human bones are preserved in the church, and there may be a connection between some legend relating to them and the Saracens' heads which form the subjects of four of the carvings. The workmanship is rough in the extreme; the flowing locks are smooth curves, hollowed here and there by the gouge, but the effect is striking.

Fig. 1. 1. A Saracen's head with a cap turned up back and front with a rose in the centre. D. & S., foliage.

Fig. 2. 2. A Saracen's head with flowing locks; the eyes are most extraordinary, without eyelids or pupils, and are probably intended to convey extreme ferocity. D. & S., foliage.

Fig. 3. 3. A Saracen's head with a turban, with eyes like those of a chameleon. D. & S., grotesque.

Fig. 4. 4. The head of a lady in cushioned head-dress and drapery. D. & S., foliage.

Fig. 5. 5. The winged lion of St. Mark, in an extraordinary attitude, holding a scroll in its mouth and paws. D. & S., foliage.

6. An angel holding an open book. D. & S., foliage.

7. A Saracen's head of similar character to the others.

IRTHLINGBOROUGH, NORTHAMPTONSHIRE.

The church was made Collegiate in 1376, the College having been founded by John Pyel, citizen and mercer of London, and in 1373 Lord Mayor Pyel, and his widow after his death, fitted the church with stalls. The College consisted of six Canons, one of whom was Dean, and four clerks.

There are eight stalls, four on each side of the chancel. They are in a bad state of repair; the elbows are carved. Only one bracket has carving, and the work is so worn that the lines are all softened away.

North Side, commencing West.

1. } *Missing.*
2. }
3. A plain bracket.
Fig. 1.   4. A demi-angel, crowned, with out-spread wings, bearing a shield, uncharged.

South Side, commencing West.

1. A plain bracket.
2. A plain bracket.
3. *Missing.*
4. A plain bracket.

Plate 30.

Fig. 4.

Fig. 5.

IRTHLINGBOROUGH.

Fig. 1.
No. 4, North.

Fig. 1.
No. 3, North.

Fig. 2.
No. 2, North.

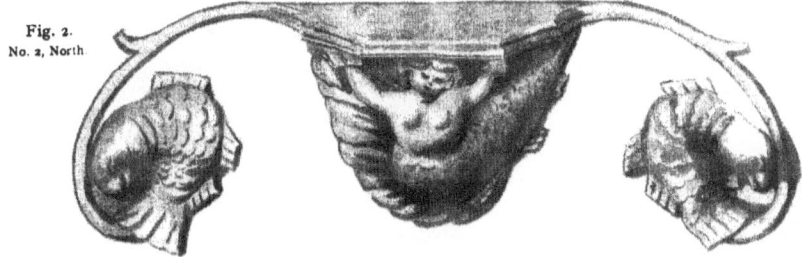

Fig. 3.
No. 1, South.

ALL SAINTS', WELLINGBOROUGH, NORTHAMPTONSHIRE.

The stalls in this church may be accounted for by the fact that the living belonged to Crowland Abbey, Lincolnshire, from a very early period, having been presented to it by Ædred, King of the Mercians, A.D. 948. The date of the stalls and misericords may be fixed within a few years by the shield carved on the elbow of the stall nearest the altar on the South Side. This shield bears a fleur-de-lys between two flaunches, each charged with a fleur-de-lys; the arms of White. Now, in the list of presentations to the living occurs the name of one John White, who was presented by the Bishop of Lincoln in the year 1361, and held the benefice till 1392. A further matter of interest attaches to this period, for in the seventh year of Richard II. (1383) four arbitrators were appointed to settle the disputes between the Abbey and its tenants, and one of the conditions of settlement was that the monks should at their own expense repair the chancel of the church. It would seem, therefore, that these stalls were erected between 1383 and 1392, the last year of John White's office as vicar. They stand three on each side of the chancel. The elbows are carved.

North Side, commencing West.

Fig. 4.   1.   A fox running away with a goose. A branch of a tree on the right. D. & S., ball of foliage.

Fig. 2.   2.   A mermaid, her tail to the left and her arms uplifted. In her right hand she holds a comb, in her left a circular mirror. The sea is represented behind on the right side. D. & S., a fish.

Fig. 1.   3.   A wood carver at work; he wears a tippet fastened with a rose-like brooch; his sleeves are puffed at the shoulders; he wears a peaked cap, hose and pointed boots. Resting on his knees is a piece of wood or bench, whereon is the boss of a rose which he is carving. On either side of this are ranged four tools, mallet, chisels and gouges. Behind him are two eagles with wings extended. Behind them again is foliage. D. & S., foliage.

South Side, commencing West.

Fig. 3.   1. A man and woman standing on either side of a table. He is dressed in a jerkin loosely laced in front, hose and boots; he scratches his head with his left hand, his right hand is broken off. The woman holds a jug in her right hand and a cup in her left. Behind them is foliage. D. & S., a rose.

2. An eagle perched on a branch, its wings extended. D. & S., small eagle.

3. Two lions advancing from either side, their heads being close together in base. Behind each is a smaller one. D. & S., small lion, *passant regardant.*

Fig. 4.
No. 1. North.

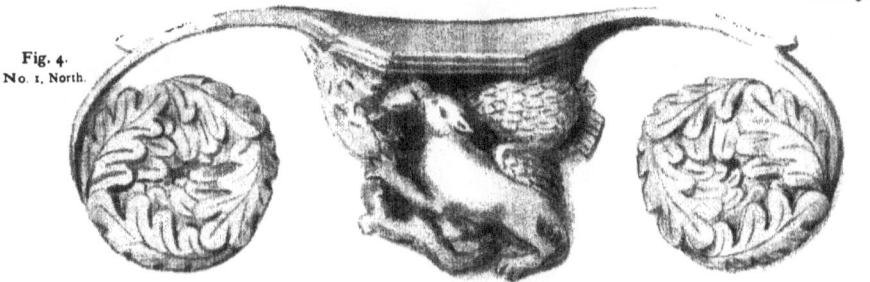

HIGHAM FERRERS.

Fig. 1.

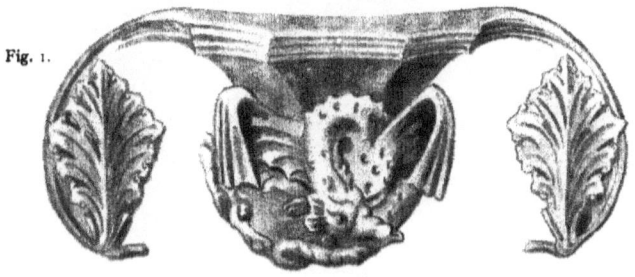

Fig. 2.

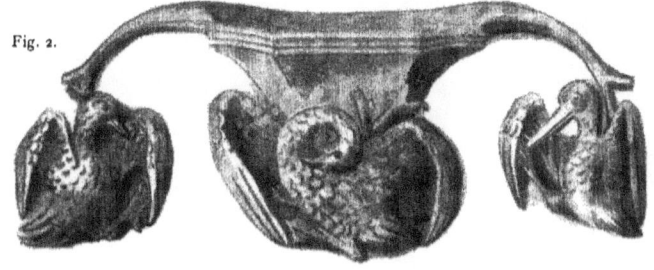

Fig. 3.

Fig. 4.

Fig. 5.

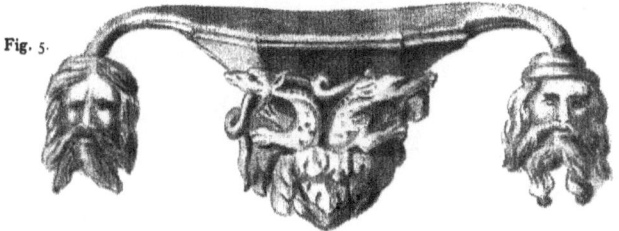

Fig. 6.

Fig. 7.

Fig. 8.

ST. MARY'S CHURCH, HIGHAM FERRERS, NORTHAMPTONSHIRE.

Archbishop Chichele attached a College to this church in 1415, the year following his appointment to the See of Canterbury. He fitted the chancel with twenty stalls for the members of the College. The elbows are carved for the most part with heads of monks and nuns. The carvings on the misericords vary in excellence, the most interesting are as follows :—

Fig. 1.   1. A soft-winged dragon, biting its tail. D. & S., well-carved foliage.

Fig. 2.   2. A swan pluming itself. D., a plover. S., a woodcock.

Fig. 3.   3. A crowned head. D., a man's face, with remarkable cap. S., a nun's head ; the drapery falls in very soft folds.

Fig. 4.   4. A lion *passant*, behind him are some very stiff trees. D. & S., foliage.

Fig. 5.   5. Two dragons, back to back, issuing from a bunch of hop leaves. D., head of a man without a cap. S., a similar head in a cap.

Fig. 6.   6. A man's head in drapery. D. & S., similar heads.

Fig. 7.   7. A head in drapery. This is probably an attempt to illustrate the legend of St. Veronica (see Subject List). D., portrait of a lady in an elaborate head-dress. S., portrait of a gentleman in a cap of peculiar shape.

Fig. 8.   8. Foliage. D. & S., foliage.

H

ALL SAINTS', LEIGHTON BUZZARD, BEDFORDSHIRE.

There are twenty-eight stalls in all, six being returned. Some of the stalls appear to have belonged to Guilds in the town, the trade emblems appearing on the elbows of the South side. They are naturally associated with the cell of Cistercian monks, which Lysons tells us existed at Leighton as an offshoot of Woburn Abbey. They appear to date from the latter part of the fourteenth century; the elbows are carved.

North Side, commencing West.

Fig. 3.   1.   A man's head, clean shaven, with curly hair. D., a shield charged : a chevron
             between three martlets, two and one. S., a shield charged with two chevrons.
         2.   A rose. D. & S., roses.
         3.   A woman's head with wimple and gorget. D. & S., leaves.
         4.   *Broken.* D. & S., leaves.
         5.   A stem between two leaves. D. & S., leaves.
         6.   A lion's mask. D. & S., leaves.
         7.   A large leaf. D. & S., small leaves.
         8.   A woman's head in wimple and gorget. D. & S., leaves.
         9.   *Broken away.*
Fig. 1. 10.   A man's head. D. & S., square foliated ornament.
        11.   *Broken.* D., a leaf. S., *broken.*
        12.   A man's head in a cap. D. & S., leaves.
        13.   A flower. D. & S., leaves.
Fig. 5. 14.   The grinning face of a man ; he wears a hood with a liripipe.

South Side, commencing West.

Fig. 6.   1.   A swan with out-spread wings. D., a shield charged with the arms of Beauchamp :
             a fess between six cross crosslets. S., a shield charged with the arms of St.
             Albans : a cross saltire.
Fig. 2.   2.   A dragon. D., a shield charged with the arms of De la Pole : a chevron between
             three lion's heads *couped* and *langued ;* a mullet *for difference.* S., the same,
             without the difference.
         3.   Two apes seated facing each other. D. & S., leaves.
         4.   A woman's head in wimple and gorget. D. & S., leaves.
         5.   Two leaves. D. & S., leaves.
         6.   A rose with sprays on either side. D. & S., large rose.

Fig. 1.
No 10, North

Fig. 2.
No. 2, South

Fig. 3.
No. 1, North

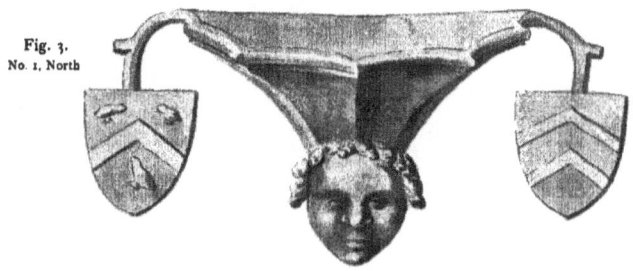

Fig. 4.
No. 8, South

Fig. 5.
No. 14, North

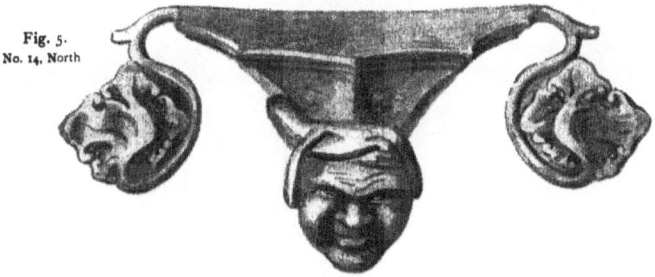

Fig. 6.
No 1, South

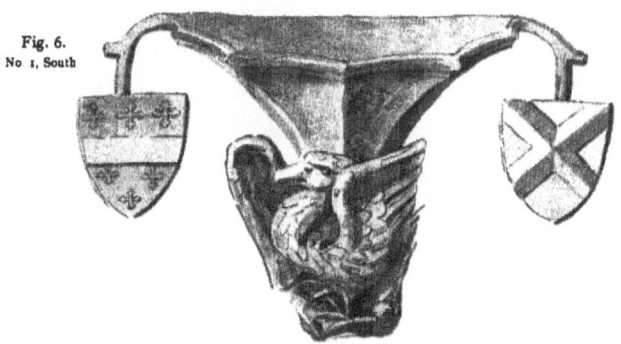

7. *Missing.* D. & S., leaves.

Fig. 4. 8. A man's head in capote and liripipe. D., a shield, charged : in chief, three annulets with a fleur-de-lys *for difference ;* on a fess, three torteaux or bezants. S., a shield, charged : *checky,* a chevron.

9. A head in a cap. D. & S., leaves.

10. A woman's head. D. & S., leaves.

11. A woman's head with long flowing hair, the tresses being brought down on either side of her face, and crossed saltire-wise beneath her chin. D. & S., rose.

12. A man's head in a hood. D. & S., leaves.

13.

14. *Missing.*

WINCHESTER COLLEGE CHAPEL.

There are eighteen stalls in the chapel, ranged against the north and south walls. Formerly the stalls extended the whole length of the chapel, but they were cleared away to give more room for the students. The woodwork of those destroyed was distributed among old Wykehamists. The elbows are carved. They date 1390.

North Side, commencing West.

Fig. 2.   1. A large dragon, with ribs strongly marked. The face finely modelled.

Fig. 5.   2. The parable of the Good Shepherd. A countryman with hat on head tied under the chin, with large laced boots, a sheep under each arm. D., a man with hood drawn over his head, a stick in his hand, standing on a spray of convolvulus. S., a shepherd running ; crook, falling from his shoulders in hand, with sheep slung over his shoulders. The robber's weapon has gone.

Fig. 1.   3. A falcon with mallard in its talons. D. & S., leaves.

4. Foliage. D. & S., leaves.

5. A dragon with out-spread wings. D. & S., square foliated ornaments.

6. Foliage. D. & S., leaves.

7. Demi-figure of a man in a high buttoned coat. D. & S., foliated masks.

8. Foliage. D. & S., leaves.

9. A foliated head. D. & S., leaves.

South Side, commencing West.

Fig. 4.   1. A cripple with clogs on his hands and knees, a pouch at his side. His feet are like hands. D., a man in hat and long cloak brandishing a falchion. S., an ape in a hood, and tight-fitting jester's dress, escalloped, fastened with numerous buttons. He carries a horn.

2. A large head with curly beard. D., a lion's mask with tongue protruding. S., the sun *in his splendour.*

3. *Missing.*

Fig. 6.   4. A human-headed dragon with out-spread wings. Over her head curves a serpent-headed tail. D. & S., conventional foliage.

Fig. 3.   5. A lion's mask with tongue protruding. D. & S., dragon curled up in a circle.

6. A large foliated head. D. & S., square foliated ornaments.

7. A pelican *in her piety.* D. & S., leaves.

8. Two goats standing on their hind legs, facing inwards, while they eat the leaves from a vine. D. & S., double-bodied dragon.

9. A man with a link in his right hand and a dagger in his left. His face shows extreme terror. He wears a quilted jerkin, and has pointed shoes. No doubt pursuing "Jack o'lantern." D. & S., sprites or Jack o'lanterns grinning at the centre subject.

Fig. 1.
No 3. North

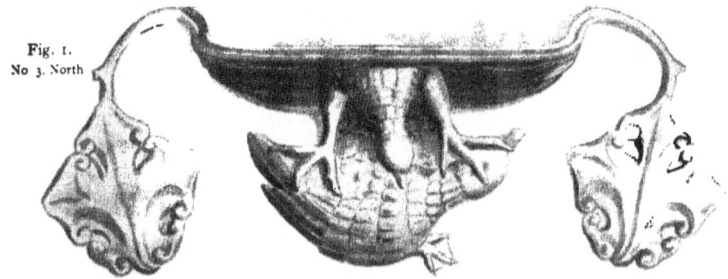

Fig. 2.
No 1. North

Fig. 3.
No. 5. South

Fig. 4.
No. 1, South

Fig. 5.
No. 2, North

Fig. 6.
No. 4, South

BRAMPTON.

Plate 39.

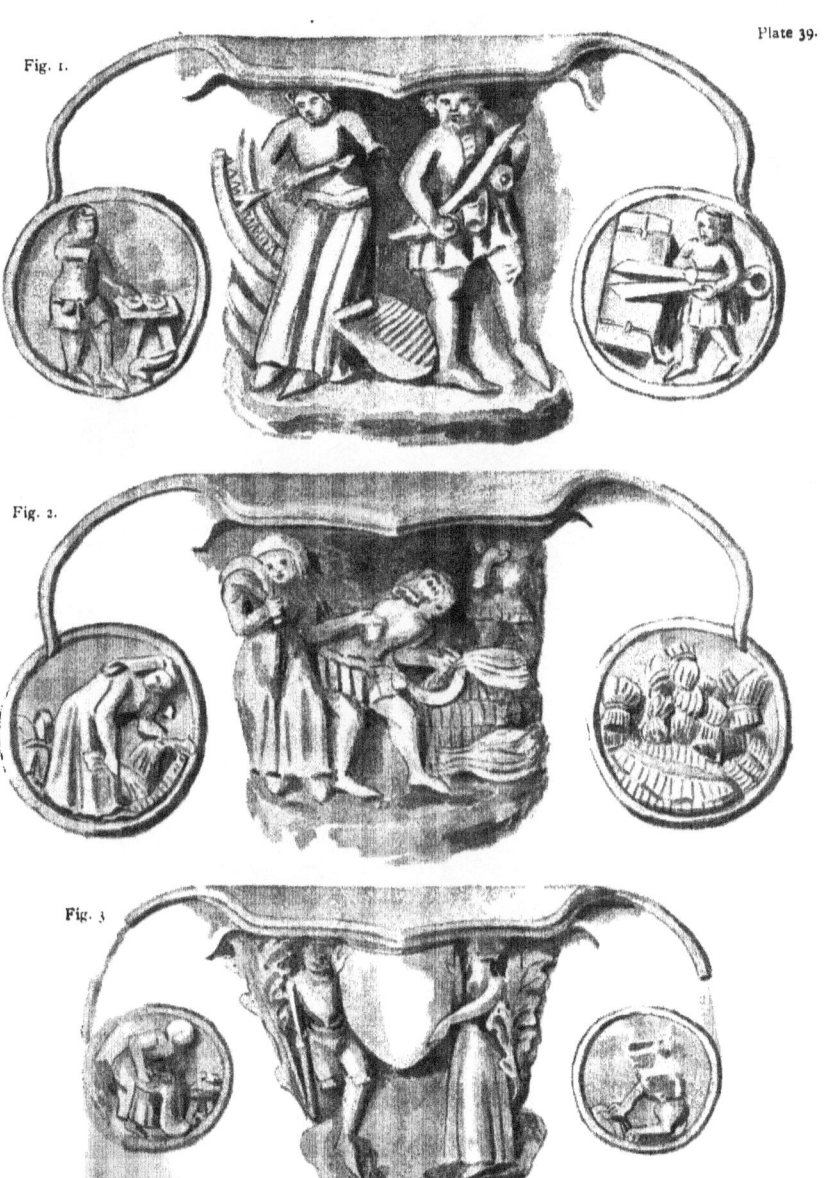

Fig. 1.

Fig. 2.

Fig. 3

BRAMPTON, HUNTINGDONSHIRE.

The following stalls were formerly in the church of Brampton, Huntingdonshire. They are of fourteenth century date. They are now in the Museum of Archæology, Cambridge.

Commencing from Left.

Fig. 3. 1. A knight and lady, bearing between them a heater-shaped shield. The knight is fully armed in the fashion of Edward III., with peaked helmet and camail; he bears a lance in his right hand. The lady, in a wimple, holds the shield with both hands. Foliage behind them. D., a man seated, a stool before him, on which rests an inkpot; he writes on a long scroll on his knees. S., a lion, *sejant*.

Fig. 1. 2. A man mowing hay with a broad-bladed scythe. He wears a tight jerkin and flat cap; the jerkin buttoned up the front with large buttons, and a gypcière hangs from his belt. He has pointed shoes. The woman draws the hay together with a large toothed rake (her arms gone). D., a carver standing at work at a bench with three legs; at his waist a gypcière and knife; he is carving with a gouge the spandril of arcading. S., a weaver standing at a table on which is fastened a length of cloth, cutting the pile with an enormous pair of scissors.

Fig. 2. 3. A man and woman reaping corn with sickles. Behind, a third figure winds a horn. D., a woman gleaning. S., a pile of sheaves.

N.B.—In all the "supporters" the moulding of the bracket is continued and surrounds the subject. The carving is much broken.

GREAT MALVERN, WORCESTERSHIRE.

The stalls are in four blocks, consisting of six stalls each. Two against the North wall and two in front of them. The elbows are carved, but are much worn. They date about 1400.

First Block: Back Row.

1. A man in an unbelted tunic, holding a spray of roses in each hand. D. & S., square foliated ornament.
2. A winged and horned monster like a cockatrice. D. & S., square foliated ornament.
3. A demi-angel playing the cithern. D. & S., square foliated ornament.
4.   D. & S., square foliated ornament.
5. A man clad in a tunic girt round the waist with a jewelled belt, standing over an ox. D. & S., square foliated ornament.
6. A beardless mask with long hair. D. & S., beardless mask.

Second Block: Back Row.

1. *Missing.*
2. A grotesque animal like an ox with tongue protruding. D. & S., square foliated ornament.
3. A cowled figure driving an evil spirit before him with a pair of bellows. D. & S., bird's heads.

Fig. 2. 4. A figure in bed, the body nude, wearing head-gear. He (or she) is supported by a nurse, behind the head. At the foot of the bed stands a man, probably the physician, clothed in a long garment with lappet sleeves, holding a bottle with his left hand and taking another such from the recumbent figure with his right. D. & S., serpent's head. [*See* SWELF, *Subject List.*]

Fig. 4. 5. A merman and mermaid. The merman holds in his right hand a mirror, the mermaid a comb. D. & S., bird's head.

Fig. 6. 6. Two monsters, back to back, *respectant.* The dexter has a human head and feet, the sinister a beast's head and human feet. D. & S., cowled mask.

Third Block: Front Row.

1. *Missing.*

Fig. 1. 2. A man clad in a tight-fitting tunic, beating down acorns from an oak ; the acorns are remarkably fine. D. & S., boar.
3. Four figures, three male and one female, intertwined so as to form a circle, while a fifth and larger figure issues head downwards from the bracket. D. & S., dragon's head.

Plate 40.

Fig. 1.
No. 2, 3rd Block

Fig. 2.
No. 4, 2nd Block.

Fig. 3.
No. 6, 4th Block

Fig. 4.
No. 5, 2nd Block

Fig. 5.
No. 3, 4th Block.

Fig. 6.
No. 6, 2nd Block

4. Two human-headed monsters, with two clawed feet. The dexter has a woman's head, the sinister a man's, their necks are crossed. D. & S., dragon's head.

5. A man kneeling on his right knee, holding a woman's right foot in his hands, her leg being raised. With his left hand he grasps the toe, and with his right endeavours to draw off the heel. She is seated and wears a long cloak with lappet sleeves, her hair bound with a kerchief. Over his head is some broken object, apparently held by the woman (no doubt a ladle)! D. & S., winged head.

6. A man in a tunic without a belt; over his right shoulder passes a strap from which depends at his left side an open box full of seed. At right stands a sack with the mouth open. His right arm is broken off. D. & S., birds flying, ready to devour the sower's seed.

Fourth Block: Front Row.

1. A demi-figure in Benedictine habit, holding in each hand a large chalice. In front of him a table on which lie certain objects, perhaps a knife and loaf. D. & S., rose.

2. A man in a tunic without a belt. In his right hand he holds a forked stick with which he holds down a plant or weed, and is in the act of cutting it off with a long handled " wedehoke." D. & S., birds.

Fig. 5. 3. Three rats hanging a cat. They pull a rope over a crossbar supported by two rough staves. The face of the cat shows sublime indifference to the proceeding. D. & S., owl.

4. A man in a short tunic with a plain belt. He holds before him a scythe. D. & S., square foliated ornament.

5. A man in a coat with eight large buttons, girt with a plain belt. On his right arm he bears a basket full of fruit, and with his left he holds up a large pear. D. & S., square foliated ornament.

Fig. 3. 6. A cockatrice. D. & S., square foliated ornament.

ST. MARY'S HOSPITAL, CHICHESTER.

There are twenty-four stalls, but only thirteen misericords. Six stalls are returned, three on each side of the entrance to the chapel which forms the east end of the Hospital. The episcopal mandate to consecrate the chapel dates 1407. Details of these stalls and pictures of the misericords are given in the *Architectural Association Sketch Book*, New Series, vol. 10. All the elbows are plain.

North Side, commencing West.

1. *Blank.*
2. Foliage (no "supporters").
3. ⎫
4. ⎬ *Blank.*
5. ⎭
6. Foliage (no "supporters").
7. *Blank.*

Fig 3.   8. A large mask, the face clean-shaven; from his eyes proceed foliage. D. & S., sun's head *in glory.*

9. ⎫ *Blank.*
10. ⎭
11. Foliage (no "supporters").
12. *Blank.*

South Side, commencing West.

1. A man in a long cloak with cap on, sprawling forward; he stands on his head, and supports the bracket with his feet. D. & S., a leaf.
2. *Blank.*

Fig. 1.   3. A double-bodied dragon, with one head. D. & S., leaves.
4. A monster, web-footed and bearded; his tail ends in a leaf. D., a man's face. S., a woman in a wimple.
5. A monster with female head. D. & S., a lion's mask.
6. A merman supporting the bracket with his shoulders; he wears a loose tunic and has a cap. With his left hand he grasps his tail. D. & S., a leaf.
7. *Blank.*

Fig 2.   8. A lion's mask, with long pointed ears. In its mouth are the tails of D. & S., which are two dragons; they bite the moulding of the bracket, which is turned down.
9. Foliage. D. & S., a leaf.
10. The demi-figure of a man, crouching and supporting himself on his hands; he has a cap on his head, and his beard is long and curly. D. & S., two dragons, their heads close to the man's beard.

11. ⎫ *Blank.*
12. ⎭

Plate 42.

Fig. 1.
No 3, South.

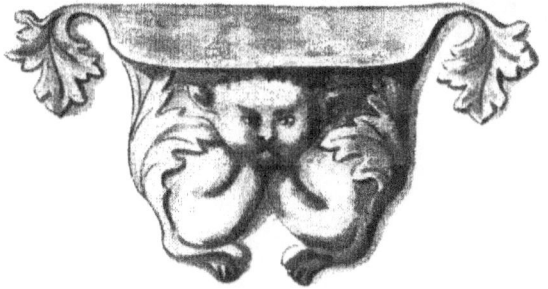

Fig. 2.
No. 8, South

Fig. 3.
No. 8, North

ST. MARY'S MINSTER, ISLE OF THANET.

There are eighteen stalls; ten on the north side of the chancel and eight on the south. On each elbow is the demi-figure of an angel wearing a coronet, which rises in front in the shape of a cross. They were erected in the time of John Curteys, Rector from 1401 to 1419.

North Side, commencing West.

Fig. 1.   1.   A female-headed winged bird, with talons; the head is surmounted with the horned head-dress of the period. D. & S., a female-headed snake, with lobster's claws, surmounted by the horned head-dress, curled in a circle.

      2.   A shield, charged with a fess between three mullets *(Manston, of Manston Court).* D. & S., leaves.

Fig. 8.   3.   An antelope, *gorged,* with collar and chain. D. & S., conventional foliage. [There is a tradition that the King granted the original foundress of the nunnery as much land as a hunted stag would go round in its course.]

      4.   A shield charged as No. 2, with a crescent *for difference.* D. & S., shield.

Fig. 2.   5.   A shield, charged : ermine, a chief quaterly *(St. Nicholas).* D. & S., a demi-angel, with remarkable head-dress, bearing shield, uncharged.

Fig. 4.   6.   A woman with huge horned head-dress, between the points of which is seated a demon. D. & S., lion's mask with tongue protruding.

      7.   Two birds, back to back. D. & S., dolphin.

      8.   An angel bearing a shield, uncharged. D & S., double rose.

      9.   A plain bracket. D & S., a four-petalled rose.

Fig. 5.   10.   A woman, seated, in the centre holding a distaff; on her right is a cat, on her left a dog, or perhaps another cat. D., a fox running away with a goose on its back. S., the large mask of a man clean-shaven.

South Side, commencing West.

Fig. 9.   1.   A demi-angel playing a cithern. D. & S., lion's mask.

      2.   A man's face, with curly hair. D. & S., dragon curled up. [As the good lady who shows you round explains, these dragons are "emblems of eternity, or a whiting dressed for dinner ! "]

      3.   The bust of a man who is laughing immoderately. D. & S., lion's mask.

      4.   A bearded head of a man with a turban. D., a demi-angel clad in feathers, round whom is a scroll inscribed **Johanes.** S., a similar angel, with a scroll inscribed **Curteys.**

I

Fig. 7.   5. A cook stirring a pot, and "shouting for more seasoning, with his hand to his mouth." Behind him is a ladle, with a shovel (or chopper). D. & S., swan on its nest.

Fig. 6.   6. Has been called "the bridled scold." The possession of a "gag" in the vestry, an instrument for suppressing a railing wife, has probably suggested this inter-pretation of the subject. It is a stern, calm face, with oak foliage issuing from the mouth. D. & S., bird on similar foliage, with scroll in its beak.

Fig. 3.   7. An archangel, clad in feathers, bearing on its breast the sacred monogram, J. H. C. D. & S., dragon curled up.

8. The head of a man with beard and long hair. D. & S., the mask of a sensual-looking monk.

Plate 43.

Fig. 1.
No. 1, North

Fig. 2.
No 5, North

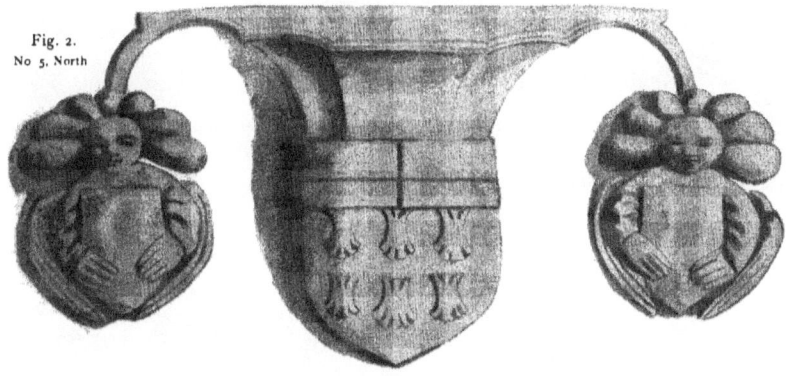

Fig. 3.
No 7, South

Fig. 4.
No 6, North.

Fig. 5.
No. 10, North.

Fig. 6.
No 6, South.

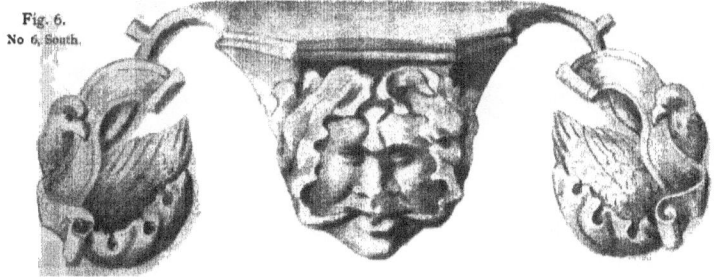

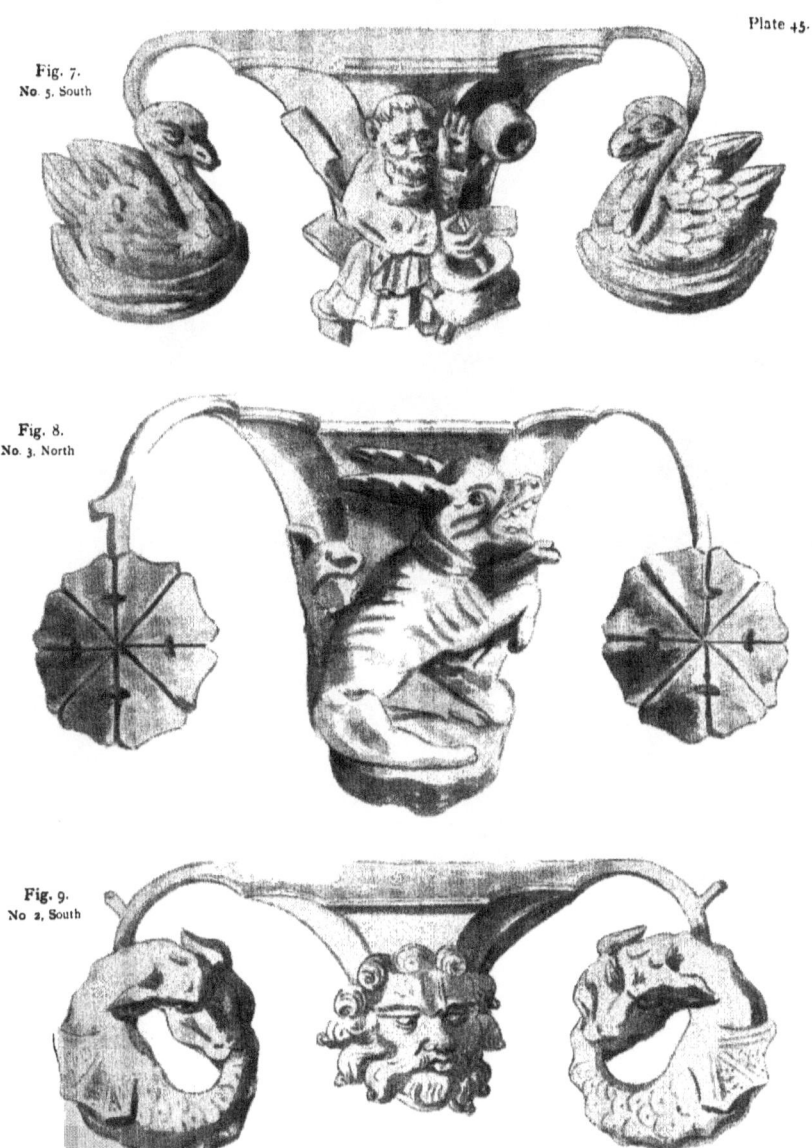

Fig. 7.
No. 5. South

Fig. 8.
No. 3. North

Fig. 9.
No 2, South

Plate 46.

Fig. 1.
No. 8, North

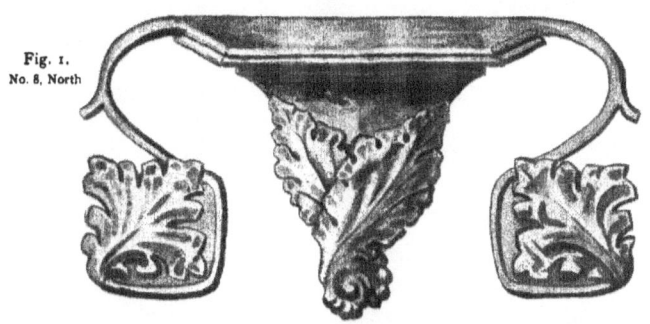

Fig. 2.
No. 10, North

Fig. 3.
No 9, North

ALL SAINTS', MAIDSTONE.

There were originally twenty-eight misericords in this Collegiate church, only twenty remain; no less than five have heraldic devices. They date early fifteenth century, as in A.D. 1395, the nineteenth year of Richard II., William de Courtenay obtained the King's license to convert the Parish church of St. Mary at Maidstone into a Collegiate church for one Master or Warden and as many chaplains or ministers as he should think fit. He gave the new church its present name. The elbows are carved.

North Side, commencing West.

1.)
2.)
3.) *Missing.*
4.)
5. A lion's head with tongue protruding. D. & S., small lion's mask, with tongue protruding.
6. A leaf. D. & S., leaves.
7. A shield, charged with the arms of Canterbury : a staff in pale, thereupon a cross *patée*, surmounted by a pall charged with four crosses *fitchée*. D. & S., smaller shield, similarly charged.

Fig. 1.   8. Two large leaves entwined. D. & S., leaves.

Fig. 3.   9. Demi-figure of a cook, a flesh-hook in his right hand, and a ladle in his left. He wears a hood and a tight jerkin, buttoned with large buttons; the sleeves of his jerkin are turned back and scalloped. D. & S., flowers.

Fig. 2. 10. Demi-figure of a boy, or angel, with cap. D. & S., leaves.

      11. Leaf. D. & S., leaves.

Fig. 6. 12. A bearded head. D. & S., leaves.

      13. A large leaf. D. & S., leaves.

      14. A shield, charged with a chevron *engrailed*, between three leaves. D. & S., smaller shield, similarly charged.

South Side, commencing West.

1. *Missing.* A correspondent to the *Gentleman's Magazine*, vol. 64, says that on the bracket of the first stall, which would be the Master's seat, was the figure of an ecclesiastic, which he suggests was Dr. John Wotton, the first Master.

2.｝
3. *Missing.*
4.｣

Fig. 5.   5.   A shield, charged with the arms of Courtenay, three torteaux, a label *for difference*, impaling Canterbury; a mitre on each point of the label. Perhaps alluding to his three bishoprics, St. David's, Exeter, and Canterbury. D. & S., leaves.

6.   A shield charged with the arms of Courtenay, with a mullet on each point of the label *for difference*. D. & S., smaller shield, similarly charged. (The arms of Edward Courtenay, the Archbishop's third brother.)

7.   Three leaves. D. & S., leaves.

8.   A shield charged with Courtenay, with a crescent on each point of the label *for difference*. D. & S., smaller shield, similarly charged. The arms of Thomas Courtenay, the Archbishop's second brother. [N.B.—A very unusual arrangement of the crescents.]

Fig. 4.   9.   A sunflower. D. & S., smaller sunflower.

10.   A large leaf. D. & S., leaves.

11.   A sunflower. D. & S., smaller sunflower.

12.   A shield, charged with Courtenay, with a torteaux on each point of the label *for difference*. D. & S., small shield, similarly charged. (The arms of Philip Courtenay, the Archbishop's fifth brother.)

13.   A large leaf. D. & S., leaves.

14.   A bearded head. D. & S., leaves.

The arms of the Courtenays are those of Godfrey de Bouillon. One of the cadets of the family who took part in the first crusade married a kinswoman of that famous warrior, and was allowed to bear the same arms, *or*, three torteaux, *gules*.

Fig. 4.
No. 9, South.

Fig. 5.
No. 5, South.

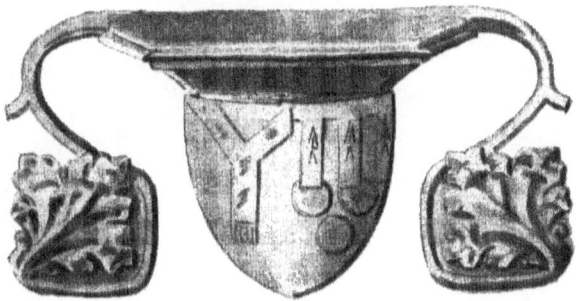

Fig. 6.
No. 12, North.

WALPOLE ST. PETER, CAMBRIDGESHIRE.

This church has been called "the Cathedral of Marshland." The misericords in the chancel are but fragmentary, except on the north side, where a few remain. They are shallow misericords and are unique in being placed under stone canopies, and in resting on stone supports; their date is 1420. The elbows are carved.

North Side, commencing West.

1. *Missing.*
2. A pelican *in her piety.* D. & S., leaves.
3. An eagle. D. & S., leaves.
4. A large head in a circle *(much broken).*

South Side, commencing West.

1. ⎫
2. ⎬ *Missing.*
3. ⎭
4. A bird (?). D. & S., leaves.

TILNEY ALL SAINTS', NORFOLK.

This is one of the many fine churches of Marshland, a few miles from Lynn. There are eighteen seats in the choir, four are returned; their date is about 1420. The carving on all the misericords is foliage, with the exception of one, which has a man's head.

Fig. 1.

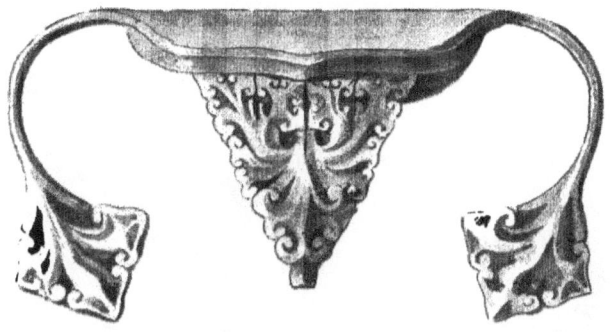

Fig. 2.

Fig. 3.

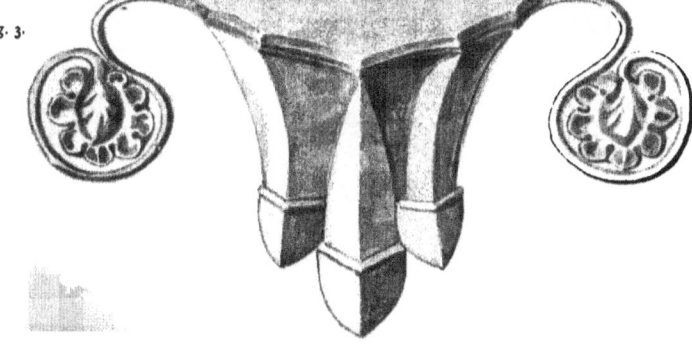

Fig. 1.
No. 8, North.

Fig. 2.
No. 3, South

Fig. 3.
No. 2, North

Fig. 4.
No. 7, South

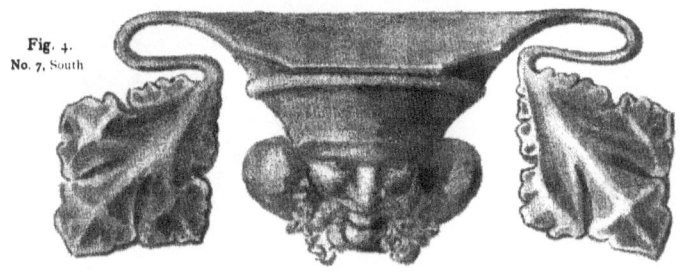

Fig. 5.
No. 4, South

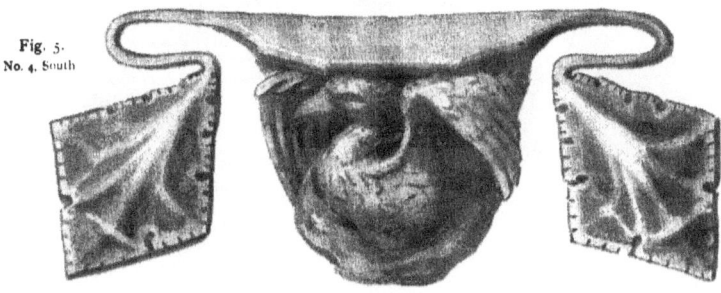

Fig. 6.
No. 5, South

ST. MICHAEL'S CHURCH, BISHOP'S STORTFORD, HERTFORDSHIRE.

There is a tradition that the misericords in this church came from St. Paul's Cathedral after the fire. The living is in the gift of the Precentor of St. Paul's and the Bishop of St. Alban's, alternately, so that if they were preserved they may have been sent here. Against this theory must be set the fact that the carving is hardly good enough for such an important edifice as St. Paul's. With the exception of No. 1, south, all the "supporters" are rather stiff leaves, some turned down, others turned up.

North Side, commencing West.

1. A monk with curly hair, holding a shield.
Fig. 3. 2. A nun in proper head-dress, with two tiny hands.
3. A man's head, clean shaven.
4. A man's head, with beard.
5. Head of a man, with beard.
6. A man's head, with drapery.
7. An eagle.
Fig. 1. 8. Head of a monk, with cowl.
9. A grotesque head.

South Side, commencing West.

1. A man's head, with curls and drapery, hands appearing beneath a band. D. & S., a small head with long hair and curls.
2. Eagle or falcon with wings expanded, bound by a strap.
Fig. 2. 3. A whale. This has been called a crocodile, but it has neither legs nor scales. It has a fine row of teeth, but so had a whale for aught the carver knew
Fig. 5. 4. A swan with upraised wings.
Fig. 6. 5. A head of a man in a turban ; curly hair.
6. Head of a man with massive curls and moustache.
Fig. 4. 7. A head of a man in a fez, with beard and prominent shoulders.
8. Man's head with curly hair.
9. An owl with out-spread wings.

ALL SOULS' COLLEGE, OXFORD.

There are forty-two stalls in the chapel, four being returned; but these are later, and have no misericords. The elbows are uncarved. They date 1442. The College was founded by Archbishop Chichele in 1437 for a Warden and forty Fellows. It is curious that the arms of Chichele do not appear on these stalls as they do at Higham Ferrers, Northants, his other Foundation.

North Side, commencing West.

1. 2. } *Blank.*

3. A man seated, his hood drawn over his head, playing the bagpipes. D. & S., rose.

4. A double-bodied mermaid with extended arms. It seems as if she had held some objects in her hands, but they are broken off. D. & S., rose.

Fig. 3.   5. A man in a belted long cloak, seated on a four-legged stool, on his head a flat cap, his left hand is held up to his ear, his right hand holds up his right leg. D., a man similarly dressed, but standing. S., the same man, apparently, holding a round target and a club.

Fig. 2   6. A man seated, with a flat cap. Round his shoulders is bound a large square pack, his hose are ungartered, and he draws on his pointed boot with both hands. D. & S., leaf.

7. An eagle with out-spread wings, holding up a scroll. D. & S., rose.

8. A lion's mask. D. & S., flower.

9. A double-headed eagle. D. & S., eagle.

10. An eagle with out-spread wings, holding in its talons the leg of some animal which it pecks vigorously; the marks of its beak are carefully carved. D. & S., lion's mask, with tongue protruding.

11. A demi-angel, bearing a crown. D. & S., square foliated ornament.

12. A head with beard and moustache. D. & S., leaf.

13. The bust of a young woman. On her head a close-fitting cap, from which her curly hair escapes on either side. A wreath of roses is hung about her shoulders. D. & S., leaves.

Fig. 1   14. A bearded posture-maker, a flat cap on his head. He lies on his back with his legs up, supporting the bracket. D. & S., leaves.

15. A lion. D. & S., leaves.

16. An owl with out-spread wings. D. & S., leaves.

Fig. 4.   17. A woman's head veiled, in a wimple. D. & S., leaves.

18. The demi-figure of a man clothed in leaves or scales. In his right hand he bears a broken falchion, in his left a round target. D. & S., shield, uncharged, depending from the moulding of the bracket.

Fig. 1.
No. 14, North.

Fig. 2.
No. 6, North

Fig. 3.
No. 5, North

Fig. 4.
No. 17. North

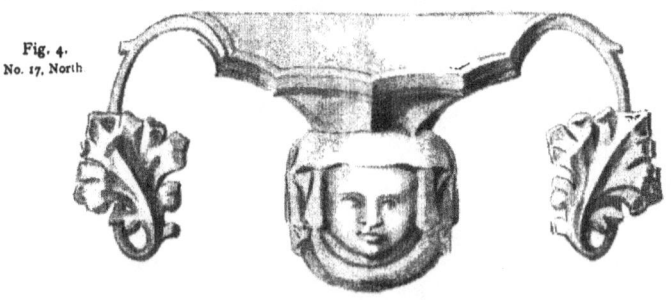

Fig. 5.
No. 14. South

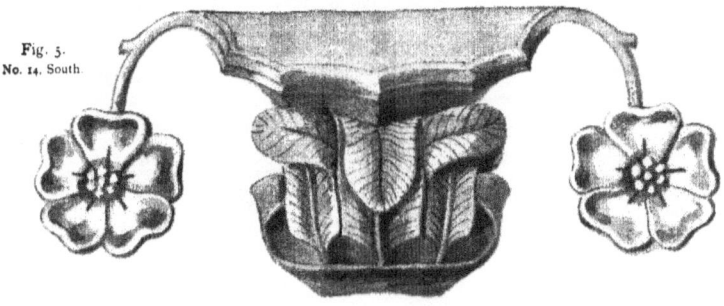

Fig. 6.
No. 3. South

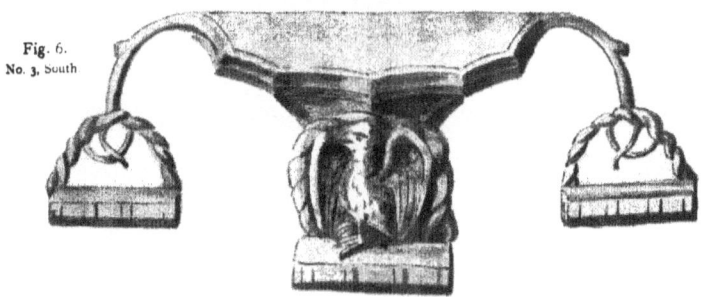

19. The bust of a man in flat cap. Round his shoulders hangs a wreath of roses. D. & S., leaves.

20. A bracket or font with arcading ; on either side issues a scroll. D. & S., square foliated ornament.

21. A queen's head, crowned. The crown is of fleur-de-lys and jewelled. A necklace of beads is round her neck, and more beads are round her hair, which is dressed in a net on each side of her forehead. D. & S., leaves.

22. A leopard or lion passant; the vertebræ of his neck are well marked. D. & S., square foliated ornament.

23. Foliage. D. & S., leaves.

South Side, commencing West.

1.
2. } *Blank.*

Fig. 6. 3. A falcon and fetterlock (the badge of the House of York). D. & S., fetterlock.

4. Two roses (?) back to back. D. & S., foliage.

6. A swan with out-spread wings. D. & S., leaves.

6. An ecclesiastic's head in a mitre. The carving of his chasuble is very fine in the undercutting (possibly *Archbishop Chichele*). D. & S., leaves.

7. A demi-angel, bearing a shield, uncharged. D. & S., heads of women in caps, their hair flowing.

8. Bearded heads of men in high hats. D. & S., head of monster.

9. A fiend's mask. D. & S., ivy leaves.

10. A griffin. D. & S., small birds.

11. A man clad in a short tunic (his head and legs broken off), holding a large hound (?) by the neck with his left hand; the sleeves of his tunic are long. D. & S., square foliated ornament.

12. A woman drawing ale into a jug from a barrel which stands on a four-legged stool. With her right hand she holds a bone (?) which she munches. D. & S., leaves.

13. A doe, behind which is a scroll. D. & S., square foliated ornament.

Fig. 5. 14. Three ostrich feathers, a scroll over their quills. D. & S., rose.

15. A dragon. D. & S., mitre, with jewelled " infulæ."

16. A large rose. D. & S., rose.

17. A tusked hart with a single horn (? unicorn). D. & S., ivy spray.

18. A wyvern. D. & S., square foliated ornament.

19. Two does, back to back, *respecting.* D. & S., ivy spray.

20. A lion's mask. D. & S., rose.

21. A woman's head in wimple, bound under the chin with a gorget. D. & S., small head of a similar character.

22. A king's head, crowned. D. & S., leaves.

23. A composite monster. It has a human head, deer's hoofs, a lion's mane, and is bearded. D. & S., four roses on a spray.

J

ST. MARY'S, BEVERLEY, YORKSHIRE.

There are twenty-eight stalls with misericords, four returned, which
are new. The lower part of most of the carvings has been carefully
restored. The date 1445 has been assigned to them from the costume
of the king in No. 10, N. The elbows are carved with winged figures.

North Side commencing West.

1.
2. } *Modern.*

Fig. 2.   3. A monkey holding up a bag to an ecclesiastic, who shows a large coin in his hand ;
behind the monkey is a man dressed in a loose fitting tunic with scalloped
sleeves, holding something like bread in his hand. D. & S., foliated face.

     4. A knight charging a dragon with his sword, another dragon lies behind him. D. &
S., a leaf with bird in centre.

     5. Two wodehouses with clubs ; on either side a dragon with his face towards the
men. D. & S., a leaf with dragon in centre.

     6. A knight attacking a wild boar nearly as tall as himself with a spear. D. & S.,
a leaf.

Fig. 5.   7. A king sitting cross-legged on a throne : his flowing mantle is scalloped. He holds
a sceptre in each hand, the one in the right is broken. A griffin, standing on
an elongated dragon, supports him on either side. D. & S., an angel in foliage
playing a cithern.

     8. A pelican *in her piety.* D. & S., a leaf.

     9. A king holding a sceptre in his right hand, with his left keeping back a man riding
on a goat, with a small dog under his arm. On the king's right is a man riding
a lion (?), forcing its mouth open. A dog under each rider.

Fig. 1.   10. A scene from *Valentine and Orson,* a romance of the period. The twins, who had
been brought up, the one by a bear, the other by a king, meet in a wood and
recognise each other. D. & S., foliated face.

     11. A head with foliage coming from its mouth. D. & S., a leaf.

Fig. 4.   12. A fox preaching in a pulpit between two monks, each of whom has a long scroll in
his hand. Below are two seated monkeys, also with scrolls. D. & S., a leaf.

Fig. 8.   13. A head with foliage coming from its mouth. D. & S., a foliated head.

Fig. 12.   14. An eagle holding an open book, from which two foxes are reading. D. & S.,
a leaf.

Fig. 1.
No. 10, North.

Fig. 2.
No. 3, North.

Fig. 3.
No. 3, South.

Fig. 4.
No. 12, North.

Fig. 5.
No. 7, North.

Fig. 6,
No. 13, South.

Fig. 7.
No. 14, South.

Fig. 8.
No. 13, North.

Fig. 9.
No. 1, South.

Fig. 10,
No. 4, South.

Fig. 11,
No. 7, South.

Fig. 12,
No. 14, North.

South Side, commencing West.

Fig. 9.   1.   A stag lying under a tree, a small dog on each side.   D. & S., a leaf.

        2.   *New.*

Fig. 3   3.   An ecclesiastic with hood and gown, holding a scroll.   On either side of him stands a fox, holding a pastoral staff, with a goose hanging out from his cowl behind. Trees in background.   D. & S., a small dog in a leaf.

Fig. 10   4.   Elephant and castle ; at sides vine leaves and grapes.   D. & S., a leaf.

        5.   A king's head between two oak leaves.   D. & S., a leaf.

        6.   A tree between two griffins, under each a rabbit.   D. & S., a leaf.

Fig. 11.   7.   A bear-baiting scene : worthy of note for "the quiet dignity of the characters concerned."   D. & S., foliated face.

        8.
           } Foliage. *New.*
        9.

       10.   A wodehouse between two lions ; dragons under his feet.   D. & S., a leaf.

       11.   A head with sprays.   D. & S., a leaf.

       12.   *New.*

Fig. 6.   13.   A fox, who is transfixed with an enormous arrow, is apparently purchasing relief for his hurt from a monkey.   Behind the fox stands a wodehouse with his bow in his hand.   D. & S., a foliated face.

Fig. 7.   14.   A head with a cap and large curls, bunches of grapes come from his mouth.   D. & S., a foliated face.

ST. GEORGE'S CHAPEL, WINDSOR.

There are ninety-eight stalls with misericords, eight of which are returned. They date about 1450, during the reign of Edward IV. Eight of the stalls were added during the reign of George I., to accommodate the additional Knights of the Garter. The following description is, for the most part, taken from that by R. W. T., in " The Sacristy," vol. i., p. 59, where a minute description of the elbows and pendants is also given.

North Side, commencing West.

1. A castle. D., two men, the upper portion of their bodies concealed by an oval erection, which has a window in the centre. S., similar to D., but only one man and no window in the frame. This seat is of a larger size than usual.
2. A mermaid, holding a circular mirror and a comb in her hands. In the background a castle with St. George's banner floating from it. D., a bird with long neck and beak, seizing a worm. S., an animal with a fish in its mouth.
3. A nude female figure holding a monk by his garment. D., a man on horseback, tilting (*broken*). S., a stag carrying under his left leg a bow, resting his right hoof on the back of a dog ; he has a sheaf of arrows in his belt.
4. Head and foliage. D. & S., a head.
5. *Missing.*
6. Samson opening a lion's mouth; a woman (? Delilah) standing near. D., two monkeys, one putting something into the other's mouth.
7. Foliage. D. & S., foliage.

Fig. 2. 8. A falconer with two hawks. D. & S., two birds.
9. A monkey, holding a dog by his chin. D. & S., foliage.
10. Foliage. D. & S., a rose.
11. Eagle and scroll. D. & S., foliage.
12. A man among foliage. D., a bird with a scroll in its beak. S., a lion and foliage.
13. Two grotesque animals. D. & S., foliage.
14. Grotesque animal seizing a dog. D. & S., foliage.
15. A griffin. D. & S., foliage.

Fig. 3. 16. A swan with three cygnets, swimming in water. D. & S., a bird pluming itself.
17. A crowned antelope, holding a scroll. D. & S., foliage.

Fig. 1 18. A dragon with his tail in a knot. D. & S., a dragon.
19. A mermaid, holding a mirror and a comb. D., a winged lion with a scroll. S., a winged ox with a scroll.

Fig. 1.
No. 18, North

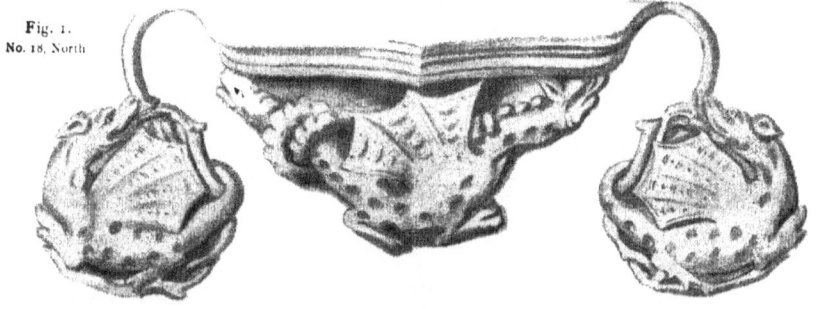

Fig. 2.
No. 8, North

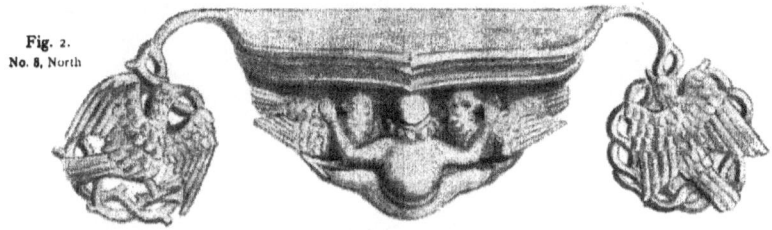

Fig. 3.
No. 16, North

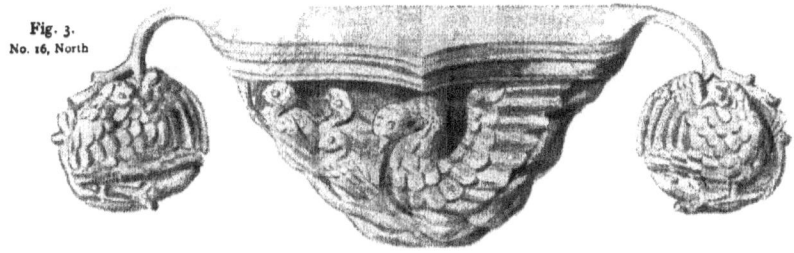

20. Foliage. D. & S., foliage.
21. A dog. D., a fox with hen in its mouth. S., a dog.
22. Grotesque face with dragons issuing from its mouth. D. & S., a rose *en soleil*, the badge of Edward IV., the "sun of York."
23. A man, ending in a fish, with a grand cap, tunic with turn-back cuffs, holding in one hand the shin-bone and hoof of an ox, in the other a circular shield with a knob in the centre. D., a bird with scroll. S., an angel with scroll.
24. Head and two small lions. D. & S., a leaf.
25. An angel holding a shield. D. & S., the same.
26. An owl, with two small birds teasing it. D. & S., two birds and vine.
27.
28. } The Royal Arms, the lion and unicorn. D. & S., an angel. *New.*

Lower Row.

1. A large bird attacking nine armed men, some of whom are wounded by it. D., a dog trampling on a dragon. S., a man driving his sword through an animal's neck.
2. An eagle seizing a rabbit; another rabbit has just run into its burrow, while others peep out from holes near. D. & S., birds and foliage.
3. Lion and unicorn. D. & S., foliage.
4. Foliage. D. & S., foliage.
5. A wodehouse attacking an animal with a club. D., an animal. S., a lion.
6. Grotesques.
7. Two demons. D., a man drinking; a demon thrusts his head into the jug. S., two grotesques.
8. A bear seizing a man by his arm. D. & S., rose.
9. A bird seizing a dog. D. & S., two deer. [This seat is now screwed down.]
10. An angel holding a scroll. D. & S., a bear and lion. [Screwed down.]
11. Two monks. D., a monkey dragging a dog by the tail. S., a monkey playing the bagpipes, another monkey blowing into one of the pipes.
12. A crown over a rose, *en soleil*, with two lions as supporters. D. & S., foliage.
13. A man with a club, holding a dragon. D. & S., grotesques.
14. A naked boy seized by two animals. D. & S., grotesques.
15. A unicorn with a magnificent tail, collared. D., a windmill; a small bird carrying a sack up the steps to the doorway; two other birds bearing sacks (?). S., an inn, with a sign hung from the side, three small birds before it. One of them offers a bowl to another large bird.
16. A face with two dragons issuing from the mouth. D. & S., foliage.
Fig. 4 17. A man lying, supporting the bracket. D. & S., a rose, *en soleil*.
18. An elephant and castle. D., two birds with worms in their beaks. S., an owl teased by other birds.

19. Two animals. D. & S., foliage.
20. Royal arms (*new*).
21. Angel and shield (*new*).

South Side, commencing West.

1. Nineteen knights, a king, and another figure (*broken*). The king seems to be starting back in surprise; the mutilated figure is holding out his hand to the king. D., a castle with moat, three knights and a king, followed by three other figures, issuing from the gateway. S., the king holding the sword and globe, surrounded by four knights, seated at entrance of the tent. This seat, as may be imagined, is of large size.
2. A castle; two soldiers looking through battlements over the gateway. D., a soldier bending a cross-bow; he holds a spear under his chin. S., soldier taking aim with a musket (?).
3. A man holding a scroll. Two birds hold the scroll at the ends. D. & S., an angel holding a scroll.
4. A jester standing before a trough, playing the bagpipes; at his right is a lady, with a dog curled up under her feet, and a hawk on her wrist. Beyond her is a hare; on the left stand a man and a dog. D., man with a long feather in his helmet, holding something. S., a squirrel, and a man with a crutch.
5. *Missing.*
6. A grotesque figure, with human head and hands, six legs, and a tri-forked tail. She, or it, holds a dragon by a rope attached to a collar round its neck. D., a dog, scratching himself with his hind foot; he has a collar to which a rope is attached. S., an elephant with a castle on his back, fastened by four straps; trees behind.
7. A mastiff and bear, quarrelling over a bone. D., an ape, holding a comb in his hand; before him is a fox seated on a stool, wearing a tippet, holding a basin in his hands, and something in his mouth. Three snails crawling on foliage. S., an ape with mouth open, seated on a stool, which has a chain attached to it; he wears a stole, and lays his hand in benediction on the head of a dog who kneels before him. Two snails in foliage.
8. Two dragons, the branches of a tree. D., grotesque animal with two horns. S., grotesque animal with one horn.
9. A fox, habited as a monk, seated in a pulpit. The head and neck of a goose peep out from his cowl behind; he holds in his hand another goose. Two others are behind him, while in front two more geese listen to his homily; towards the right a monkey with a cross-bow takes aim at him from a vine. D., a grotesque figure, the upper part a man, holding a sword and shield, trampling on a dragon. S., a man with a javelin among oak foliage.

Plate 58.

ST. GEORGE'S CHAPEL.

Fig. 4.
No 17, North
Lower Row

Fig. 5.
No. 19, South

Fig. 6.
No. 16, South

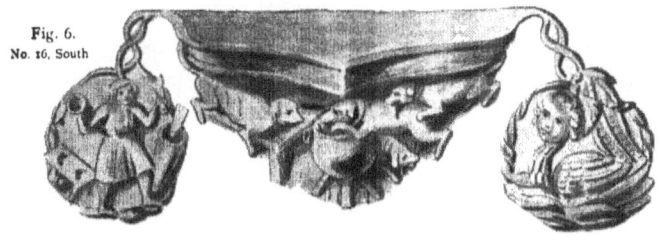

10. Two men wrestling in foliage. D., a large vase, or font, with two workmen (?) near it ; one has a hammer. Two snails in foliage. S., another large vase, with two workmen. Two snails in foliage.

11. Two dragons fighting in foliage. D., animal licking its back, which a toad is biting. S., a dog seizing a monkey, who stands at the foot of a tree.

12. Two dragons ; below them a mask. D., a dragon. S., a lion with human face and hands, and bull's horns.

13. Foliage. D. & S., foliage.

14. Three heads with beards. D., a face among foliage. S., the same.

15. A nude female figure seated on a bed, holding a monk by his robe ; a small bird between them. Towards the right behind the woman, a dove and foliage. D., a rhinoceros, with a piece of rope round his horn. S., a dog biting his tail.

Fig. 6. 16. A dog taking meat out of a pot on the fire ; three other dogs trying to get it. D., a cook holding in his left hand a knife (*right arm broken*). Behind him is a table with two platters on it and a kettle beneath it ; a pestle and mortar stand in front. S., a swan with human face.

17. A man riding on an animal like a unicorn, round whose neck is a collar with pendant in front. Facing him is a woman astride a similar animal. Behind them is a town. D. & S., foliage.

18. A face with branches coming from the mouth. D. & S., grotesque animal.

Fig. 5. 19. A mermaid, with a dragon's tail, and another figure, partly human, quadruped and fish, which holds a fish in its left hand. D., a woman's head. S., a man's head.

20. A demi-figure with jester's cap and hood. D. & S., rose.

21. Grotesque. D. & S., grotesque.

22. A unicorn trampling on a dragon. D., grotesque animal. S., a wodehouse.

23. Two grotesque animals. D., a bird. S., a bird seizing a worm or serpent.

24. Two small monkeys on a vine. D., a small monkey astride a larger, beating him with his tail. S., a grotesque animal seizing a man who is carrying something.

25. A monkey and a lizard on a branch. Two monkeys at the foot of the tree. S., two grotesque animals, one with a man's face, at the foot of a tree, on which is a snail.

26. Foliage with snails. D., a greyhound. S., a unicorn scratching its horn.

27. Royal arms. (*New.*)

28. Angel with shield. (*New.*)

Lower Row.

1. A demon pushing a wheelbarrow, in which are three monks and a fox with a goose in his mouth, into Hell-mouth. D., a man making a bow, his left hand pressed on his heart (*broken*). S., a man about to strike another with his sword.

2. Two men kneeling. A monkey astride a dog, holding up his tail and beating him ; the dog's head is turned round and he is biting the monkey's back. S., a starved dog or fox, lying on his back ; at his side is a monkey pouring water or food into his mouth from a bowl ; another monkey standing near holds a bottle in his hand, probably the doctor prescribing remedies.

3. A lion fighting a dragon. D., a wodehouse standing among vine leaves and grapes. S., the same (*broken*).

4. A grotesque animal with his paw on a dog ; behind is a wodehouse, holding in one hand a club and with the other seizing the creature by the tail. D. & S., foliage.

5. A monk seated at one end of a table on which is a dish containing food ; he holds in his hand a short rod with a knob at the end, which rests on the dish. Before him is a large jar. At the end of the table stands a demon clutching the dish. D., a grotesque figure holding a staff. S., a man with the legs and tail of an animal, walking ; in his right hand is a staff ; over his shoulders a sack, the contents of which are running out from the neck in front.

6. A man lying on his back, held down by two men ; a third is forcing a toad into his mouth. D. & S., foliage.

7. A king seated on a throne, at his left is a table on which are flagons and cups, beneath it is a trunk with a semi-circular lid. Death, represented as a skeleton, seizes him by his arm. Behind Death are two small houses. D., a man digging ; Death places his hand on his head. S., Death touching a man on the shoulder (*broken*).

8. A dog seizing a hare, and a fox running away with a goose. D. & S., foliage.

9. A man seizing a bear by the tail. The bear seems to have slipped his muzzle which hangs round his neck, and to have overturned a large jar. D., a man seated, before him a dog seated on his hind legs. S., a sow playing the harp which is suspended from her neck with a broad ribbon. Three young pigs dance to the music [Screwed down].

10. St. George and the dragon ; behind the knight kneels the princess leading a dog by a string. A king and queen look down from the wall of a city behind. D. & S., three snails crawling over a mitre [Screwed down].

11. Two men carrying rabbits. D., a pelican *in her piety*. S., a man and woman in spiral shells.

12. Lion and unicorn. D. & S., foliage.

13. A dog chasing a hare outside a park paling ; under the dog is a snail and under the hare a frog. D., a dog scratching its ear. S., a beaver. [There is a beaver on one of the elbows, so this may be a local subject.]

14. A pedlar lying on the ground at the foot of a flight of steps which lead up to a castle. Five monkeys come from the trees and pillage his pack ; one monkey has a club in his hand, and three combs lie on the ground. D., a man. S., a jester holding a bauble.

15. Two lions. D., a human-bodied figure with sword in his hand holding a dragon by the tail. S., a woman nude to the waist, carrying in her right hand a club and in her left holding up a small dog by its tail.
16. A monkey with small shield and dagger, attacking a dragon. D. & S., a grotesque.
17. A dragon seizing a lion. D. & S., foliage.
18. A man and woman quarrelling over backgammon ; behind the man is a cat, behind the woman a bottle. D., two men bound with cords. S., two men seated (*broken*).
19. Foliage with snails.
20. Royal arms (*new*).
21. Angel holding shield (*new*).

THROWLEY CHURCH, NEAR FAVERSHAM, KENT.

There are four misericords in this church.   They date 1450, and have not been renovated.

1. A boy riding on an animal with a collar, pursued by another boy; *both broken.*
    D. & S., a dragon ; its tail a continuation of the bracket moulding.
2. Foliage ; rough, but effectively carved.
3. A winged creature, pursuing a boy. D. & S., a grotesque animal of a Dachsund nature.

Fig. 1.

Fig. 2.

Fig. 3.

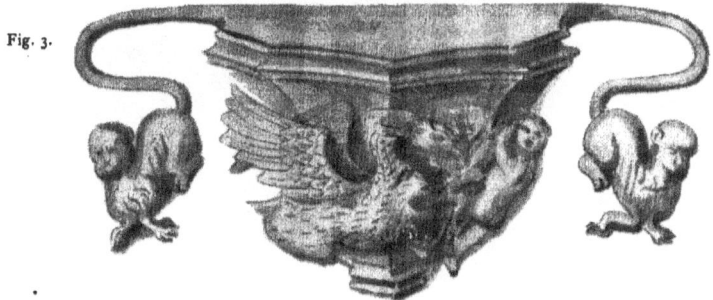

NEW COLLEGE, OXFORD.

The stalls are sixty-two in number; of these, eight are returned. The misericords were, until the restoration of the chapel in 1880-81, under the reading-desks, forming a cornice. They were then, however, restored to their original position. The College was founded for a Warden and seventy Fellows, by William of Wykeham, Bishop of Winchester, in 1386. Carvings date 1480; they are very good, and highly finished.

North Side, commencing West.

1. A double-bodied lion, crowned (*new*).

Fig. 2.   2. Three men. The one in the centre is unarmed, in both senses, and wears his hair long; he is clad in a tight-fitting tunic and pointed shoes, as are the others, with very droll effect. The man on his right (A), has in his uplifted right arm a dagger; the man on his left (B) grasps the hilt of a sword merely, the broken blade lies on the ground; with his left hand he makes a gesture of despair. D., a man with a two-handed sword advancing against (A). S., a man, nude but for a short cloak and a peaked cap, his back turned to the spectator, throws back a Roman-looking sword to strike (B).

3. A woman seated, with a distaff. Behind her, an immense cat, looking over her shoulder; behind it again, a house. D. & S., dragon.

4. A fiend seizing a man by the skirt of his tunic; the man holds a small staff. D. & S., a square foliated ornament.

5. A grotesque head of a demon, with wings sprouting from his forehead. D. & S., dragon.

6. A head, the hair foliated. D. & S., single oak leaf.

7. A large bearded head. D. & S., two oak leaves.

8. Two birds in foliage. D. & S., single large leaf.

9. Foliage. D. & S., single leaf.

10. An old man, in a long hooded cloak. D. & S., oak leaves and acorns.

11. A head of a demon, winged. D. & S., single large leaf.

12. A buck enclosed in a park, chased by a hound. D. & S., lion's head in leaves.

13. A winged scaly monster with a large moustache, having a serpent in its mouth. D. & S., face in oak leaves.

14. A rose tree in blossom; through the leaves appear the face and arm of a diminutive man. A bird lodges in the lower branches. D. & S., roses and buds.

Fig. 1.　15.　Two dragons fighting, well carved. D. & S., head with enormous crown.

16.　Foliage. D. & S., leaves.

17.　An ogre, his hands in large gauntlets, drawing four rams into his lap. D., bean stalks, which a small woman cuts with a sickle. S., bean stalks, the branches of which a small man holds with his hands ; below him is a ram.

18.　A large leaf. D. & S., large leaves.

19.　A grotesque foliated head. D. & S., leaves.

20.　A dragon in foliage. D. & S., square foliated mask.

21.　A castle gate and portcullis. D., a man's head in a peaked helmet, to which camail is rivetted. S., a man's head in a peaked helmet, to which camail is laced.

22.　A rose. D. & S., rose.

23.　Foliage. D. & S., leaves.

Fig. 3.　24.　A seven-headed dragon, or hydra ; probably intended to represent the seven deadly sins. D., a suppliant kneeling before a seated monk clad in a gown, the hood of which is being drawn over his head by a small imp ; the imp stands on the suppliant's head. S., a man stripped to the waist, wielding a knife in one hand and a scourge in the other.

25.　A shield, charged; a fess, six cross *crosslets*, three and three. D., a shield, charged : a fess, three bulls *passant*, two and one. S., a shield diapered, on a bend three popinjays.

26.　A fiend's mask, foliated. D. & S., square foliated ornament.

27.　A ram's head. D. & S., ram's head.

28.　A king's head, crowned. D. & S., human-headed wyvern.

29.　A bearded head. D. & S., large leaves.

30.　A lion's mask. D. & S., escallop shells.

31.　A large eagle, with a scroll in its mouth. D., an eagle seizing a hare by the ears. S., an eagle with a scroll.

South Side, commencing West.

Frontispiece.　1.　A cathedral city surrounded by a wall, with gate and portcullis. On the drawbridge a bishop in his mitre, holding a pastoral staff, is preaching to the monks on the dexter side. D., the heads of four monks in foliage listening to the bishop. S., the heads of five ecclesiastics in foliage ; one has on a cardinal's hat, another bears a crozier. The centre figure has his hand raised in the act of benediction. The faces have great individuality of character, and were probably portraits.

2.　A fiend's head. D. & S., square-shaped leaves.

3.　Foliage. D. & S., fleur-de-lys.

Fig. 8.　4.　An old woman's head in a high head-dress. D. & S., vine leaves.

Fig. 1.
No. 15, North

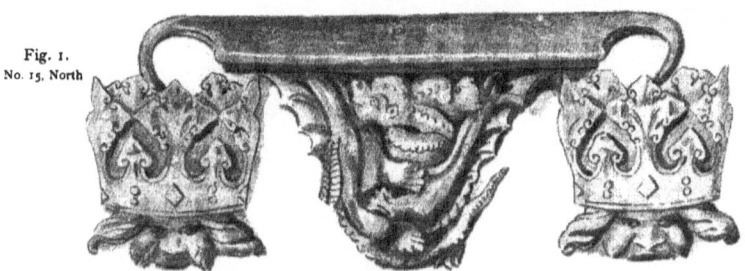

Fig. 2.
No. 2, North

Fig. 3.
No. 24, North

Fig. 4.
No 5, South

Fig. 5.
No. 14, South

Fig. 6.
No. 18, South.

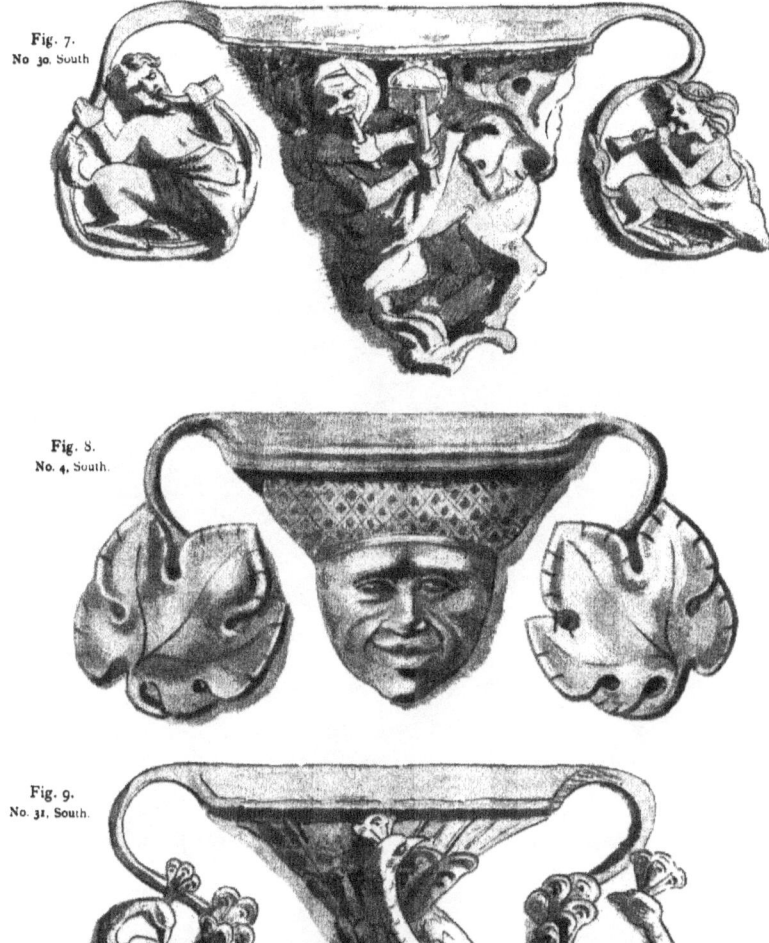

Fig. 7.
No 30. South

Fig. 8.
No. 4, South.

Fig. 9.
No. 31, South.

Fig. 4. 5. Two old women seated in a pew; in the centre, standing behind them, is a fiend with butterfly wings, who brings their heads together. D., a woman kneeling, a pair of crutches under her arms, and telling her beads. S., a monk bending forward, fast asleep.

6. Foliage. D. & S., grotesque.

7. Foliage. D. & S., lion's mask.

8. Foliage. D. & S., square foliated ornament.

9. A rose tree. D. & S., branch of three roses.

10. A quadruple man with two heads; a third head between them. D. & S., leaves.

11. An imp holding some money bags. D. & S., leaves.

12. An oriel window, latticed. D., a lattice window. S., a lattice screen.

13. A large head. D. & S., leaves.

Fig. 5. 14. A dragon. D. & S., leaves.

15. A swan with out-spread wings. D., a bird. S., a bird swallowing some small object.

16. A man in a cloak. D. & S., leaves.

17. A monkey in a cowl, issuing from a whelk-shell. D., a monkey seated on a lily. S., a monkey in a hooded cape.

Fig. 6. 18. A gateway with a portcullis, a horse and his rider passing through; the horse's hind legs alone are visible. D., a gate surmounted with a flagstaff and flag, on which is blazoned a chevron; above the battlements appears the watchman's head. S., the same, but with the flag blazoned with a cross *saltire*.

19. Foliage. D. & S., foliage.

20. A large head. D., a man's head bound with a fillet. S., a woman's head bound with circlet.

21. Foliage. D. & S., foliage.

22. A head. D. & S., square foliated ornament.

23. Foliage. D. & S., foliage.

24. An ecclesiastic preaching in a pulpit; two small figures behind him, on either side, holding staves; a small figure below him holds a book. D., a man with staff and pack. S., a beggar pointing to his feet.

25. A female centaur holding an axe. D. & S., swine.

26. A head. D., a man, armed *cap-à-pie*, holding a wyvern. S., a wyvern.

27. A female bust, with large beads round her neck. D. & S., rose.

28. Foliage. D. & S., foliage.

29. A foliated head. D. & S., rose *(new)*.

Fig. 7. 30. A centaur playing a pipe and beating a tabor. D., a centaur blowing a horn. S., a centaur playing the pipe.

Fig. 9. 31. A peacock *in its pride*. D. & S., a peacock, standing on a snake, pluming itself.

GAMLINGAY, CAMBRIDGESHIRE.

In the parish church there were six misericords, but the carving of two has been cut away. They are roughly carved, but the seats are elaborately moulded, and belong to the fifteenth century.

Fig. 1.   1. A head, which may be meant for a lion, but which is punctured all over, somewhat like a leopard. D. & S., small rose.

Fig. 2.   2. A small hooded figure, like a dwarf, with his hands raised as if supporting the bracket, which, however, he does not touch. D. & S., conventional foliage,

Fig. 3.   3. A grotesquely carved ape, with his hands behind his ears. D. & S., conventional foliage.

4. A solid mass of vine leaves and grapes, roughly carved; the veins in the leaves are mere cuts, but the effect is rich. D. & S., conventional foliage.

In this series the form of the seats and the curve of the bracket stems are of more interest than the carvings.

Plate 63.

Fig. 1.

Fig. 2.

Fig. 3.

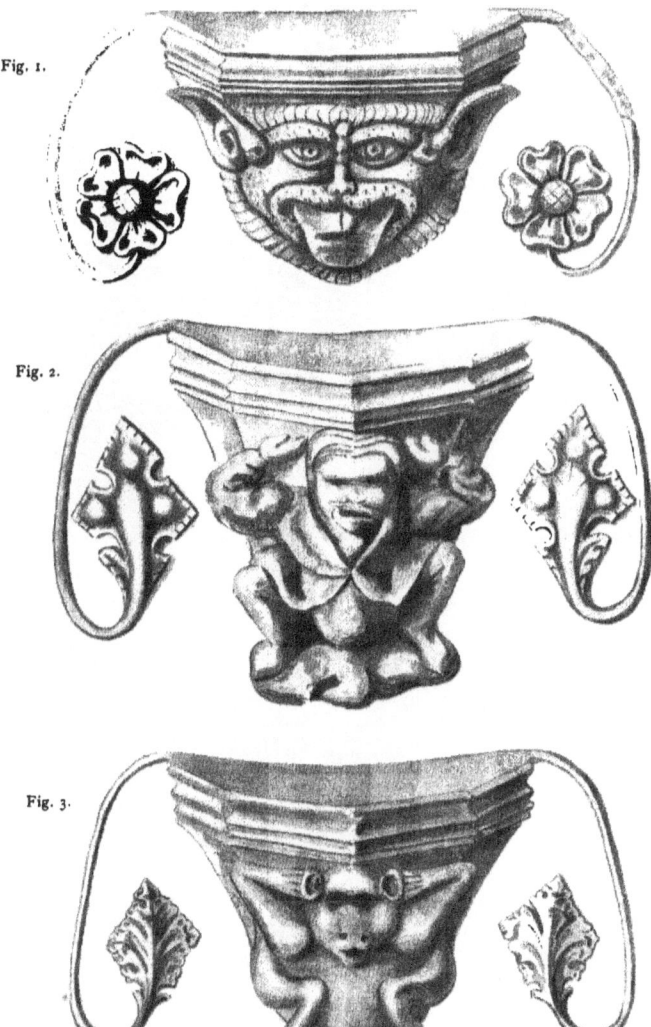

Plate 64.

Fig. 1.

Fig. 2.

Fig. 3.

BAKEWELL CHURCH, DERBYSHIRE.

There are twenty stalls with misericords in the chancel, six are returned. Only three seats are old, they date fifteenth century. The modern ones date 1881.

The Old Seats.

1. A human-headed dragon. D., a woman's head. S., a man's head in a cap.
2. Two grotesque animals, sitting together like a pair of love birds. D. & S., conventional foliage.
3. A winged dragon. D., a human-headed grotesque. S., a mermaid holding a mirror.

ST. MARY'S CHURCH, SWINE, YORKSHIRE.

The church was attached to a priory of Cistercian nuns. There were originally sixteen seats with misericords for the Prioress and fifteen nuns; only nine now remain. No "supporters." Date, fifteenth century.

North Side, commencing West.

1. A bearded man, with his legs thrown up, like No. 14, north, All Souls' College, Oxford.

Fig. 3. 2. A man's head with a forked beard.

Fig. 5. 3. A bird-lion biting its tail.

Fig. 2. 4. A knight's head in helmet, with pointed beard.

South Side, commencing West.

Fig. 4. 1. A nun's head between two creatures, back to back. Her veil is drawn half across her face, and discloses as near an approach to a wink as can be perpetrated in wood. This may have been a portrait of one of the sisters, and the fun caused by his "merrie geste" must have been the carver's excuse for introducing it.

Fig. 6. 2. A grotesque with human face and bishop's mitre.

3. A head with foliage coming from the mouth.

Fig. 1. 4. A female head in head-dress of the period.

One seat is nailed down at the back of the pulpit, too low for inspection.

Fig. 1.
No. 4, South.

Fig. 2.
No. 4, North.

Fig. 3.
No. 2, North.

Plate 66.

Fig. 4.
No. 1, South.

Fig. 5.
No. 3, North.

Fig. 6.
No. 2, South.

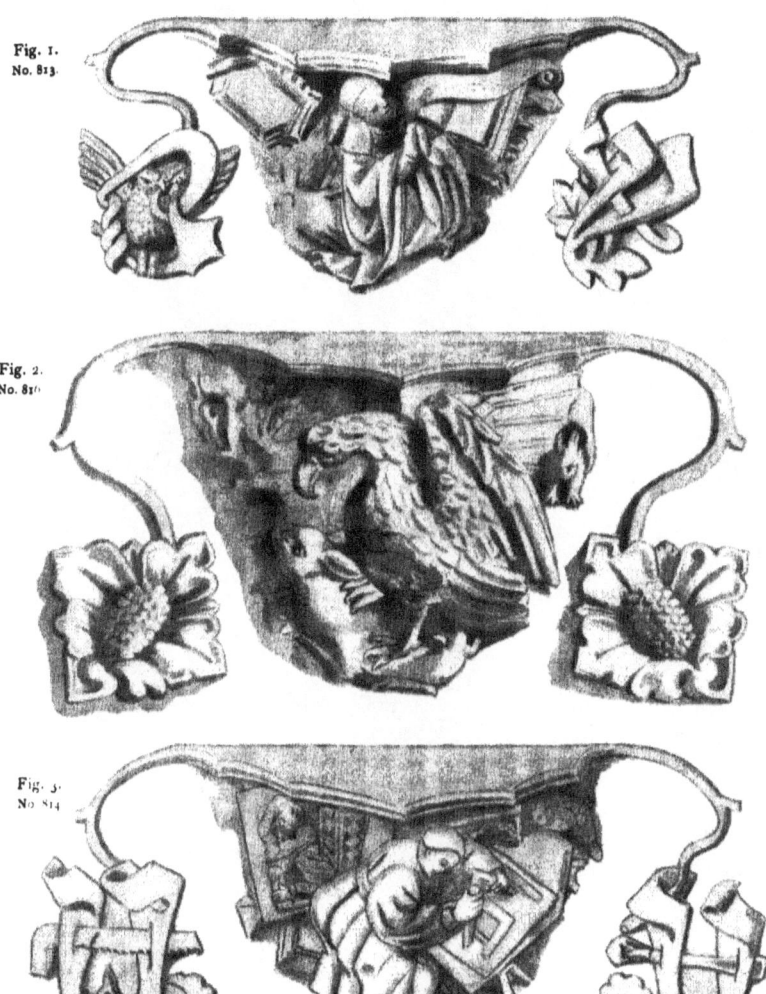

Fig. 1.
No. 813.

Fig. 2.
No. 816

Fig. 3.
No. 814

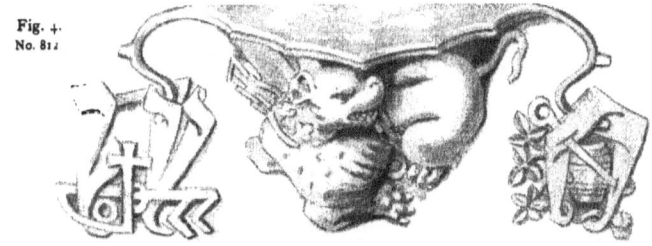

Fig. 4.
No. 81_

Fig. 5.
No. 817

Fig. 6.
No. 815.

Fig. 7.
No. 861.

Fig. 8.
No. 863

Fig. 9.
No. 862

ARCHITECTURAL MUSEUM, TUFTON STREET, LONDON.

The first six of the misericords here described were formerly in the chapel of St. Nicholas, Lynn; but on its restoration (!) in 1852 they were placed · in the hands of the contractor by the parochial authorities, and sold by him. It is to be hoped that they will no longer be moved about. They appear to be fifteenth-century work.

Fig. 4. 812. A dragon or lion *gorged* and chained. D., a merchant's mark in initials. S., a tun, flowers and leaves in an initial.

Fig. 1. 813. An ecclesiastic praying at an altar on which is laid a book, behind is a sedile. D., an eagle in a letter. S., a floriated letter.

Fig. 3 814. A carver at work, at his feet lies a dog; two apprentices at work at a bench behind him and one before him. D., an initial and a saw. S., an initial and a gouge.

Fig. 6. 815. A stag hunted by hounds. At the side is a rabbit in its burrow. D., a hunter's horn in a letter. S., a merchant's mark in a letter.

Fig. 2. 816. An eagle with a rabbit in its talons. Two young rabbits come out from their burrows in dismay. D. & S., foliage.

Fig. 5. 817. A fat, chubby-faced lion, *couchant regardant*. This has been copied on the renovated front of Westminster Abbey. D. & S., Tudor rose.

This is a very fine set indeed.

The following are originals, but the place from which they came is unknown.

Fig 7. 861. Two men in short tunics, threshing wheat with two flails. D. & S., the lower halves of two men, whose faces are in their breasts, from the back of which depend tails.

Fig. 9. 862. A man loading a farm-cart with sheaves, which are passed up to him by a woman on a fork or pole. The horse harnessed to the cart looks back at them in a very comical manner. D. & S., grotesque bird; its neck and head set on man's shoulders, drapery covers the joint.

Fig. 8. 863. A man piling sheaves in "shock." A woman brings two more to him. Her attitude is graceful. D. & S., grotesque figure.

864. An eagle with wings extended, holding a scroll. D. & S., grotesque bird.

L

GAYTON, NORTHAMPTONSHIRE.

There are six stalls in the chancel of the church, containing misericords, three on each side, none are returned. The elbows are demi-angels. They are interesting from the number of sacred and legendary subjects included in them. They are of Perpendicular date.

North Side, commencing West.

Fig. 2. 1. St. Ursula standing in the centre in a long flowing robe, fastened at the waist with a rose-brooch ; her robe is held out on either side, under which four small figures, nude, two on each side, kneel and cling to her hem. Clouds surround the saint's head. [This graceful figure may be intended for Charity.] D. & S., flowers and foliage, delicately carved.

Fig. 1. 2. Combat of a lion and dragon over a small animal, perhaps the lion's cub. D., a human-headed four-footed monster, holding a fish in its claws. S., a dragon curled up.

Fig. 4. 3. A large figure with outspread wings, clad in feathers, a shield on his right arm, and an object like the head of a rake on his left wing, seated astride two small figures. The heads of these two meet in base. The dexter wears a long robe and a flat cap ; the sinister a short tunic and flat cap, and holds a rosary. D., an ape. S., a man wearing a short tunic buttoned up the front. He kneels before some broken object. A cushion is behind him and at his left side is a hammer.

South Side, commencing West.

Fig. 3. 1. The three Marys. Three figures in long robes, seated beneath arcading. Clouds above their heads. Over the central figure is a broken object (? an angel's head). D. & S., crown ending in escallop shell from which issues foliage.

Fig. 5. 2. The Last Judgment. Our Lord seated on a throne, on either side of which rise four small figures. Those on the sinister are enclosed in a chain cable and are being dragged into the mouth of Hell, which is represented, as usual, by a pair of large jaws with sharp teeth, flames issuing from the throat. D. & S., sunflower and leaves.

Fig. 6. 3. Absalom riding through the wood of Ephraim (2 Samuel xviii, 9). Absalom, in a long cloak, his hair hanging down his shoulders but cut square on the forehead, is seated on a mule, passing through a wood. Above, David is seen seated, uncrowned, between the two gates. His hands are clasped in prayer. The mule is saddled and bridled. D. & S., grapes and leaves.

NOTE.—There is nothing to explain the presence of misericords in this church. Two of the seats (Nos. 2 and 3) are apparently of fourteenth century work, very similar to those in St. Katharine's Hospital. It seems not unlikely that a rector of the church at some time became possessed of these two seats, and gave an order to a local carver to increase the number. The other four are scriptural subjects, and are quite unique in shape ; probably of a much later date.—E. P.

GAYTON.

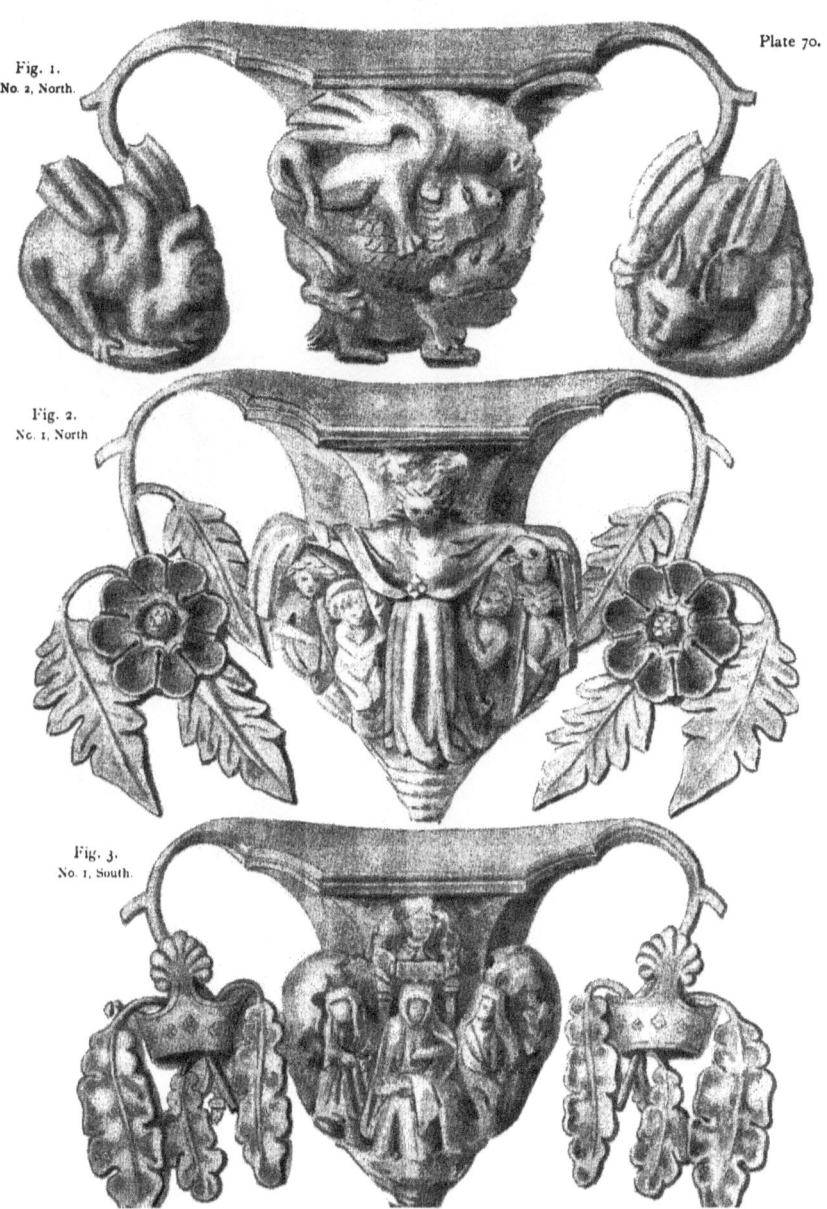

Plate 70.

Fig. 1.
No. 2, North.

Fig. 2.
No. 1, North.

Fig. 3.
No. 1, South.

GAYTON.

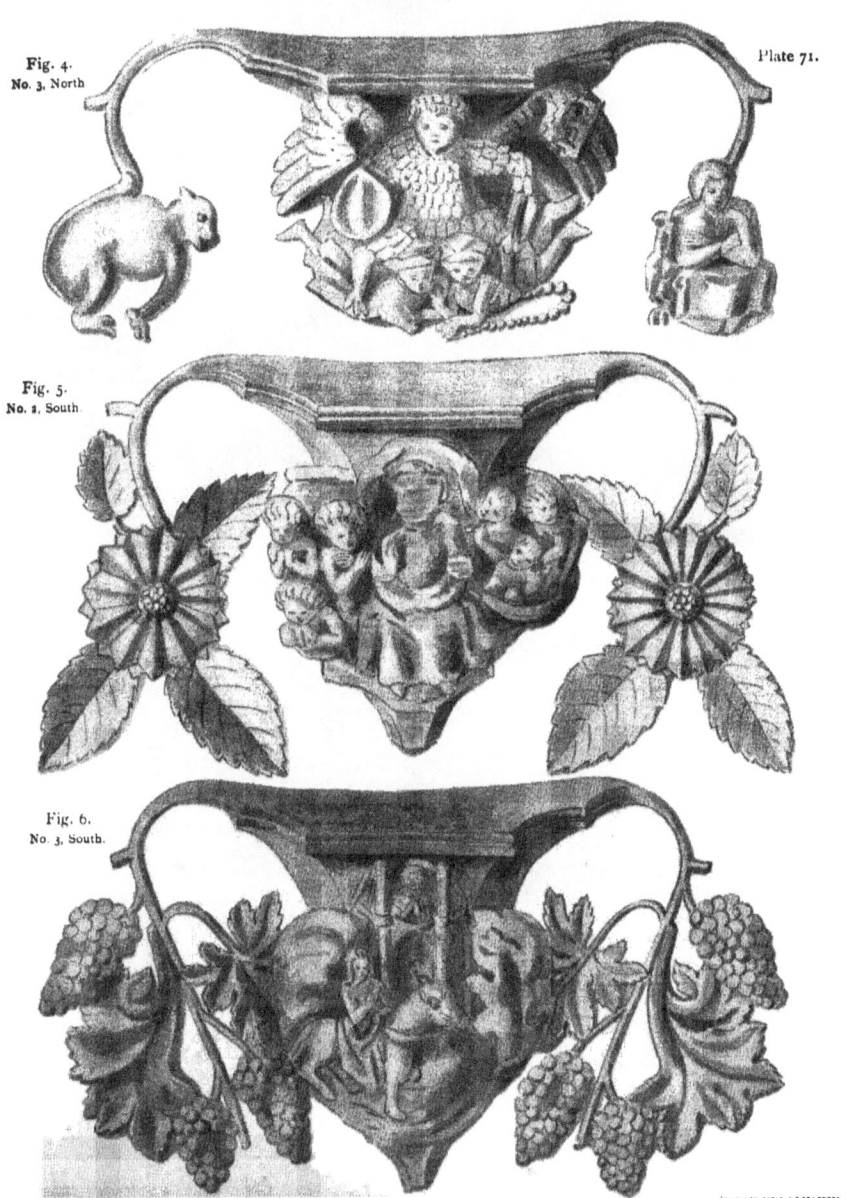

Fig. 4.
No. 3, North.

Plate 71.

Fig. 5.
No. 1, South.

Fig. 6.
No. 3, South.

INS PHOTO. SPRAGUE & CO LONDON

Fig. 1.
No. 1, South

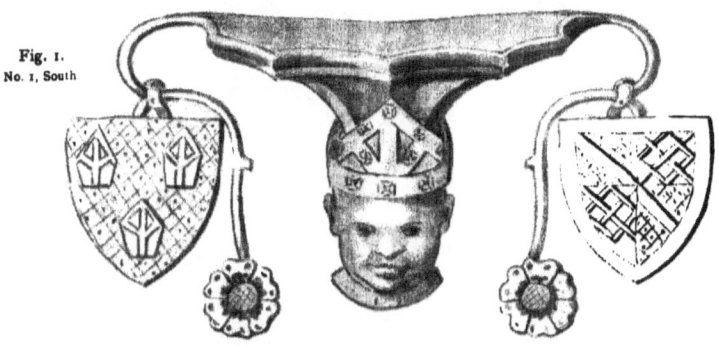

Fig. 2.
No. 1, North.

Fig. 3.
No. 5, North.

Fig. 4.
No. 5, South

Fig. 5.
No. 2, North.

Fig. 6.
No. 8, North

ST. MARGARET'S CHURCH, LYNN.

This church was at one time attached to the Bishopric of
Norwich. There are sixteen stalls with misericords of fifteenth century
date. The curves of the bracket mouldings are unusually long and
graceful. The elbows are carved.

North Side, commencing West.

Fig. 2. 1. Head with wreath. D. & S., flower.
Fig. 5. 2. Head with cap. D. & S., leaf.
      3. Man's head. D. & S., foliage.
      4. Foliage. D. & S., flowers.
Fig. 3. 5. Arms of Scales, a shield, charged with six escallop shells. D. & S., a five petalled
         flower.
      6. Head of an old man, with arms and hands below the bracket. D. & S., flowers.
      7. Foliage. D. & S., a large leaf.
Fig. 6. 8. Head of an old man, with arms and hands raised to support the bracket. D. & S.,
         foliage.

South Side, commencing West.

Fig. 1. 1. Head of a bishop in a mitre. D., a shield, charged with three mitres. S., a shield,
         charged quaterly: 1 and 4, diapered, a bend; 2 and 3, a fret, all within a
         bordure.
      2. A crowned head. D., a shield, charged with three ostrich feathers, two and one.
         S., a shield, charged, diapered, six water bougets (?), three, two, and one.
      3. Spray of flowers. D. & S., flower.
      4. Foliage. D. & S., flower.
Fig. 4. 5. Front view of a figure with bent head, with right hand supporting the bracket, left
         hand down.
      6. Face with foliage proceeding from mouth. D. & S., a leaf.
      7. Foliage. D. & S., a leaf.
      8. Head with crown or cap. D. & S., foliage.

ST. PAUL'S, BEDFORD.

There are eighteen stalls remaining of the original twenty, but they are all much broken. They are all of the same date, with the exception of two which are finer and more delicately carved. Six are returned; the elbows are carved. The two fine ones are early fifteenth century.

North Side, commencing West.

1. }
2. } *Broken away.*

3. *Broken.* D., a monkey on a leaf; in its right hand a strong staff, with which it supports itself; round its neck is a broad collar to which a small one on its back holds on with both hands. S., a monkey seated (its head gone); on its back a young one's head appears in a small circle above its shoulder; the circle, presumably, is the swathing band round the head.

4. *Broken.* D., a shield depending by a strap and buckle from the bracket moulding, charged: diapered, a cross engrailed. S., a shield similarly hung, charged: three bezants.

5. *Broken.* D. & S., leaves.

6. *Broken*, with the exception of what appears to be the end of two infulæ, the ends of which are fringed. D. & S., lion's masks with tongues protruding.

7. }
8. } *Broken away.*
9. }

South Side, commencing West.

1. }
2. } *Broken away.*

Fig. 3. 3. Foliage *(broken).* D. & S., flattened-out dragon, with ribs and vertebræ very prominent.

Fig. 2. 4. A square castle, with four round towers at the four corners in tiers, machicolated and pierced with loop-holes; in the centre of the building a gateway with portcullis. On the left of the subject an attempt has been made to give a view of the side in perspective. D., a knight armed *cap-à-pie*, his helmet pointed with camail attached, holding in his left hand what appears to be an arbalest or cross-bow; his left foot is thrust through the stirrup at the head of it. The bow and windlass are broken. S., a wodehouse looking back at the knight; in his right hand he bears a club, in his left a pointed shield, charged; diaper, a cross fleury.

　　　NOTE.—This misericord is the arms of Bedford town, the two side subjects forming the supporters of the shield; whether correctly or not, I do not know.

Fig 1. 5. Vine leaves and grapes. D. & S., three leaves forming a circular ornament.

6. A large foliated mask, the lower jaw and teeth only remain. D. & S., leaves.

7. A bearded head in kerchief *(broken).* D. & S., leaves.

8. }
9. } *Broken away.*

Fig. 1.
No. 5, South.

Fig. 2.
No. 4, South.

Fig. 3.
No. 3, South

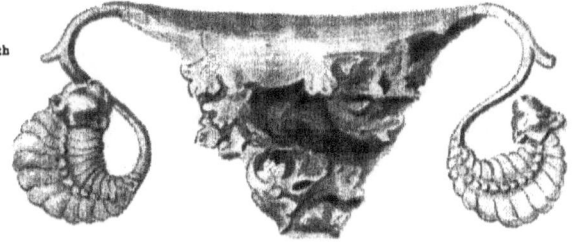

Plate 75.

Fig. 1.
No 2.

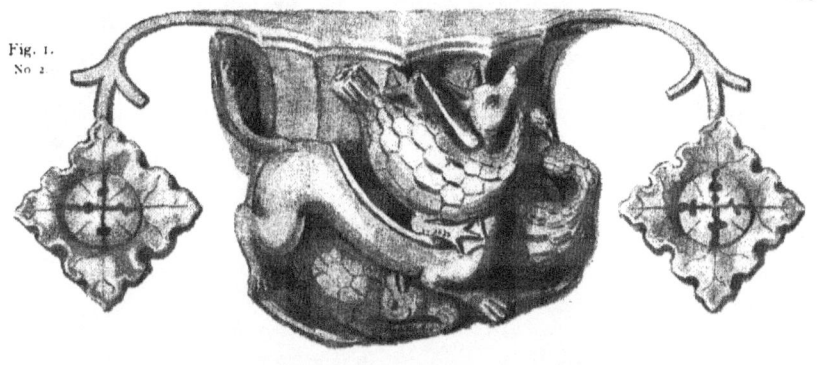

Fig. 2.
No 6.

Fig. 3.
No 1

Fig. 4.
No. 10.

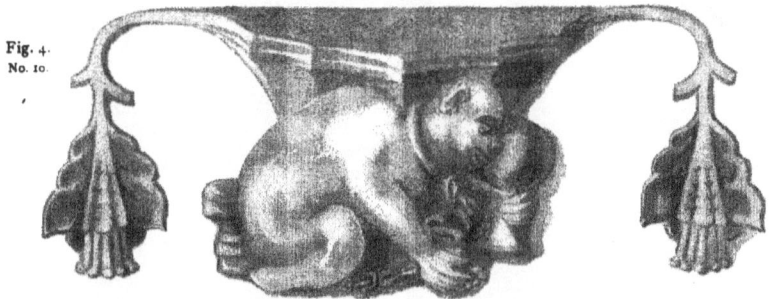

Fig. 5.
No. 8.

Fig. 6.
No. 3.

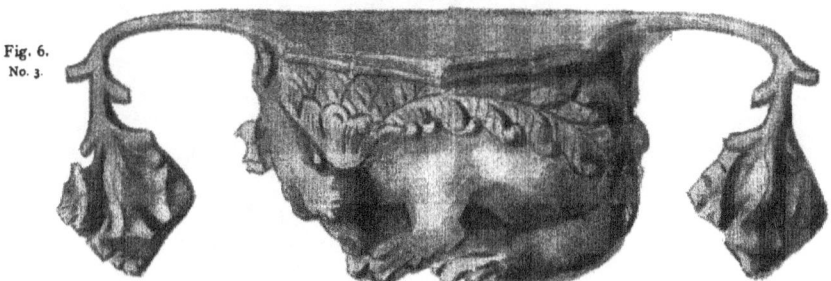

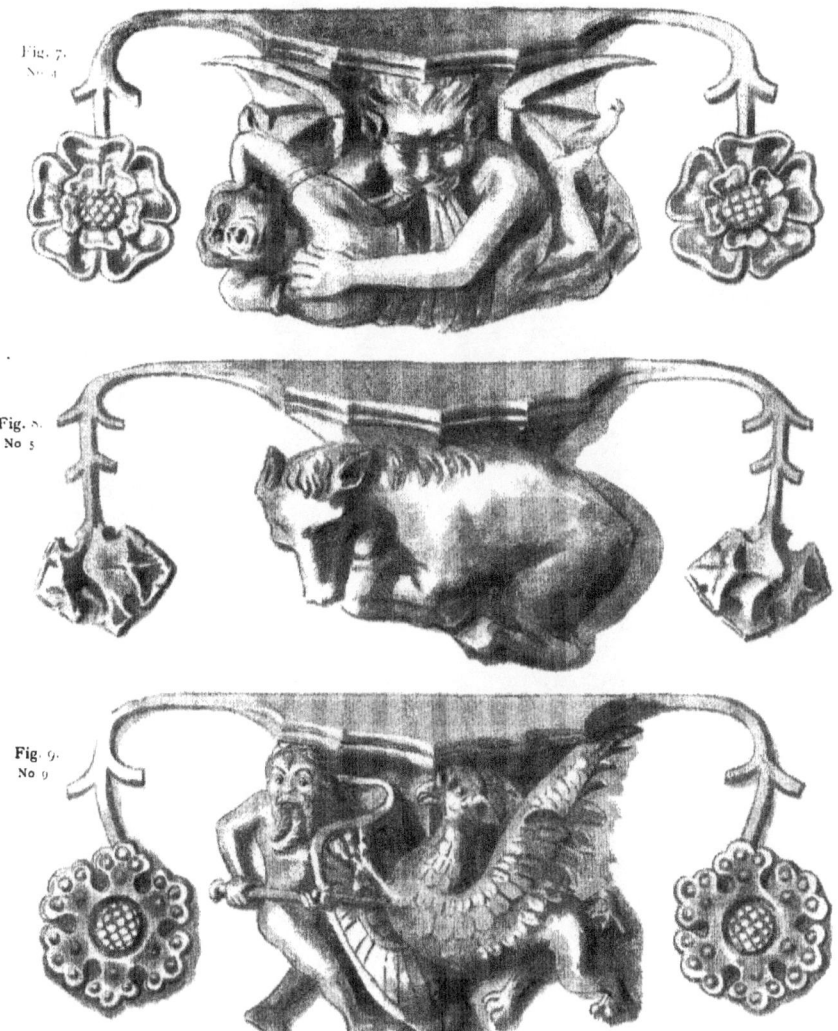

Fig. 7.
No. 4

Fig. 8.
No. 5

Fig. 9.
No. 9

FAVERSHAM, KENT.

In 1070 William I. gave the church of St. Mary of Charity and the tithes to St. Augustine's Monastery, Canterbury. There are sixteen stalls, dating about 1533; they have all been renovated, and four are modern, the work of a Pole in 1874. The carving of the new seats is very fine, and quite in the spirit of the older examples; the elbows are well carved.

Fig. 3. 1. A creature like a lioness, lying down, with a mysterious bunch of curls over its back. D. & S., flat round ornament (*modern*).

Fig. 1. 2. A fine fox carrying off a goose on his back, while two other victims lie under his feet. D. & S., foliage; four leaves spread out, four small leaves folded to the centre.

Fig. 6. 3. An animal not hitherto identified by science, licking its fore-foot. D. & S., conventional foliage.

Fig. 7. 4. A demon carrying off a lost soul; very boldly carved in high relief. D. & S., Tudor roses (*modern*).

Fig. 8. 5. A horse lying down; it does not fit the position well. D. & S., conventional foliage.

Fig. 2. 6. A triple face; either a device to represent the Trinity or the Three Wise Men. The faces and hair are of an Oriental type. D. & S., pretty conventional foliage.

7. The fable of the fox and the grapes. There does not appear to be any reason why the fox should not devour the coveted fruit, but we must not be too critical in these matters. D. & S., conventional ornament (*modern*).

Fig 5 8. A man playing the flute. The work here is so sharp that it is difficult to believe that it is four hundred years old; it may have been touched up. D. & S., conventional foliage.

Fig. 9. 9. A wodehouse behind an enormous shield, attacked by a griffin. D. & S., conventional ornament (*modern*).

Fig 4. 10. An ape attached to a post by a strong chain; he holds an empty bottle upside down in evident disgust at finding no contents. D. & S., conventional foliage.

11. A juggler.

12. Angels and figure.

13. Man with bough of tree.

14. Man and shield.

PETERBOROUGH CATHEDRAL.

Three misericords, removed from the old stalls, are standing (1895) in the south aisle, nailed on to a board, one above the other, in the order drawn. Date, fifteenth century.

1. A popinjay or pigeon. D. & S., foliage.
2. A fox seizing a fat goose by the neck and running away. D. & S., a cock with spurs.
3. A head, bearded. D. & S., a shield, uncharged.

Fig. 1.

Fig. 2.

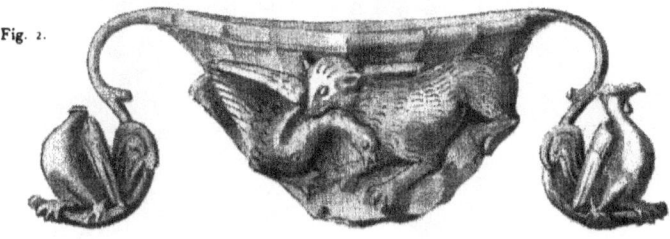

Fig. 3.

Fig. 1.
No. 4, North.

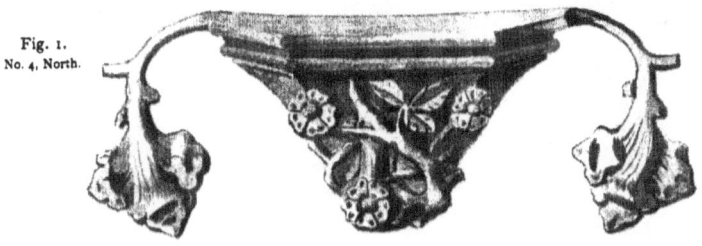

Fig. 2.
No. 5, South

Fig. 3.
No 7. North

ST. MARY'S CHURCH, RICHMOND, YORKSHIRE.

There are sixteen stalls, eight on each side.   They are late, perhaps early sixteenth century, and were brought from Easeby Abbey at the Dissolution.

North Side, commencing West.

1.
2. } *New.*

3. A grotesque mask with tongue protruding.   D. & S., a leaf.

Fig. 1. 4. A spray of roses with flowers and leaves.   D. & S., a leaf.

5. A dragon (?) carrying a goose by the neck.

6. A grotesque animal, crowned, crouching.

Fig. 3. 7. A basket of flowers.   D. & S., foliage.

A cockatrice.

South Side, commencing West.

1. Fruit and foliage.

2. A hart, *lodged, gorged*, and chained.

3. A pig playing the bagpipes, and two small ones dancing.

4. A man's head in a cap.

Fig. 2. 5. A dragon.   D. & S., foliage.

6. A dragon.

7.
8. } *New.*

MANCHESTER CATHEDRAL.

There are thirty-six stalls with misericords, six being returned. They occupy nearly three bays at the west end of the choir. The stalls were erected by Bishop Stanley, *circa* 1508, who built the new choir in 1483. The stalls on the north side were erected by Richard Beck, a merchant of Manchester. The elbows are carved.

North Side, commencing West.

1. A demi-angel, with extended wings, bearing a shield charged with the cross of St. George, the arms of London. D. & S., fir cone or pine apple.
2. A pelican *in her piety.* D. & S., chestnut leaf.
3. Two dragons fighting. D. & S., sunflower.
4. A man pursued by another man, clad in short tunic, holding a staff. (*Much broken*). D. & S., vine leaves.

Fig. 6.   5. A woman following a man, between them a pot of liquor overturned, the contents running out. D. & S., well carved columbine.

6. A dragon biting its own back. D. & S., leaves.

Fig. 1.   7. A demi-figure of a child issuing from a spiral shell, driving his spear into a dragon which attacks him. D. & S., three sunflowers.

8. Two men playing tric-trac or backgammon on a board lying between them. On either side of them a figure reclining, one playing a musical instrument, the other drawing ale from a barrel a good deal broken. D. & S., Tudor rose.

Fig. 2.   9. A wood with birds perched in the trees. Through the wood runs a hound ridden by a fox. Over the shoulders of Master Reynard a pole or staff, from which is suspended a hare. D. & S., flowers.

10. A hound pulling down a stag in the forest. The stag's tongue hangs out; some of its antlers are broken. D. & S., sunflowers.

11. A huntsman disembowelling a stag, which with cut throat lies on its back. D. & S., sunflowers.

12. (*Broken.*) D. & S., fir cone.

13. A cock and cockatrice. D. & S., flower.

14. An antelope or unicorn, *couchant*, in a wood. D. & S., rose, back view.

Fig. 3. 15. Has been called "the hare's revenge.' A huntsman bound to a pole used for a spit, which is being turned before a large fire by a rabbit or hare, whose head is lost. Four pots stand over the fire, three of which are covered, but the lid of the fourth is raised by a hare, disclosing the head of a hound, being boiled as a relish. From the huntsman's belt hangs a bugle. His legs and arms are crossed and bound to the pole by cords. D. & S., rose, side view. This finial and the last closely resemble two at Ripon.

Plate 80.

Fig. 1.
No. 7, North.

Fig. 2.
No. 9, North.

Fig. 3.
No. 15, North.

Plate 81.

Fig. 4.
No. 7. South

Fig. 5.
No. 8, South.

Fig. 6.
No. 5, North.

Fig. 7.
No 5, South.

Fig. 8.
No. 4, South.

Fig. 9.
No. 10, South.

Plate 83.

MANCHESTER CATHEDRAL.

Fig. 10.
No. 2, South.

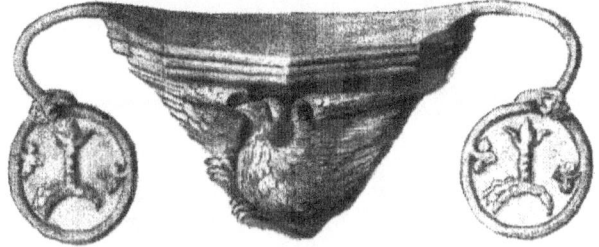

Fig. 11.
No. 1, South.

Fig. 12.
No. 3, South.

South Side, commencing West.

Fig. 11. 1. The Lathom legend. Three woodmen with wallets and axes over their shoulders hastening towards a castle, while a fourth is knocking at the gate to inform the inmates what has occurred. Tall trees, one of which contains the eagle's nest, in which lies the child in swathing hands. On the infant is perched the eagle. D. & S., leaves.

Fig. 10. 2. An eagle flying with out-spread wings. D. & S., the arms of Sir John Stanley, natural son of the Bishop, viz., an eagle's leg with talons.

Fig. 12. 3. A dragon, well carved. D. & S., fruit with triple stem.

Fig. 8. 4. A demi-angel, *volant*, bearing shield charged with the arms of the Isle of Man, viz., three legs conjoined, armed and spurred. The angel wears a loose surplice, round the neck is an amice, the collar of which may be seen distinctly.

Fig. 7. 5. An elephant, on whose back is bound a double-turreted castle, passing through a wood. D. & S., sunflower.

6. Two wodehouses, the dexter mounted on a camel, the sinister on a unicorn, fighting. D. & S., fir cone.

Fig. 4. 7. A fox with a goose in its mouth, running away from a farm-house. In the doorway stands the good wife, whose child endeavours to pull her back by the skirts of her dress. D., a fox on a stool teaching two cubs to read; a birch is held significantly over his shoulder. S., a fox seated on a stool, holding an open book between his fore legs.

Fig. 5. 8. A pedlar lying asleep; while thus unconscious a troop of monkeys rifle his pack of its contents. D., an ape holding up a bottle. S., an ape nursing a child in swathing bands, or not unlikely a baby doll from the pack, which would of course be dressed as a human baby of the period.

9. A bear collared and chained, baited by five dogs. While the bear seizes one dog two hold him by the neck and two by the haunches. D. & S., sunflowers.

Fig. 9. 10. A lion, *couchant regardant*, with a magnificent tail. D. & S., roses and buds.

11. A lion and dragon fighting. D. & S., lion's mask.

12. A wodehouse, round whose waist is a wreathed belt, armed with a shield and club, fighting a dragon. D. & S., leaves.

13. A boar on its hind legs playing the bagpipes, to the music of which four young pigs are dancing behind the trough. D., a boar playing the harp. S., a boar, round which is strapped a pack-saddle.

14. An antelope, *couchant regardant*. D. & S., flowers and fruit.

15. A griffin with wings outspread. D. & S., three flowers.

M

CHRISTCHURCH, HANTS.

There are fifty-eight stalls in this fine old Priory church, but the number of misericords is much fewer. As the brackets were not fixed to the seat, no less than twenty-six have been taken away by " person or persons unknown." The whole of the upper row on the south side has thus disappeared. Six stalls are returned. With the exception of three the misericords are all of the sixteenth century, having been erected by William Eyre, who was Prior in 1502-1520. The carving is in the Italian style. The supporters, in all cases, except the fourteenth century misericords, are conventional foliage round a piece of diaper work. The elbows are carved.

North Side, commencing West : Upper Row.

1. A grotesque face, to which are attached large ass's ears, surmounted by much drapery. The hands are in front and the mouth is gaping. The lower jaw is broken away.
2. A grotesque demi-figure of a man clad in a slashed doublet and puffed sleeves, laughing immoderately. His hair is curly and his hands hold a ribbon which passes behind his back. The ribbon is ornamented.
3. A man clad in a long loose garment, beneath which show the soles of his feet, kneeling, with his back supporting the bracket. In his right hand he grasps a large hammer or mallet, and in his left a chisel.
   Fig. 3.
4. A demi-figure with large foliated mask, the arms extended outwards, the hands grasping the foliage of the " supporters."
5. A man on his knees and elbows, supporting the bracket with his back. His doublet is turned up, showing his trunk-hose pierced for fastening with a "point," which is shown in position. His wrist bands are tight, and he holds a bowl in his hands.
6. A grotesque figure in a long cloak with large face and ass's ears. In his right hand he holds a fool's bauble with pointed ears and belled hood ; in his left he holds a roll of parchment or short staff.
7. A bat with out-spread wings and open mouth.
8. A jester sitting sideways, his left leg stretched out in front and his arm beneath it, holding the thigh ; his shoes have broad toes. A hound, whose head and shoulders only are seen, seizes the toes of his left foot.

Fig. 1.
No. 11, North

Fig. 2.
No. 4, North.
Lower Row.

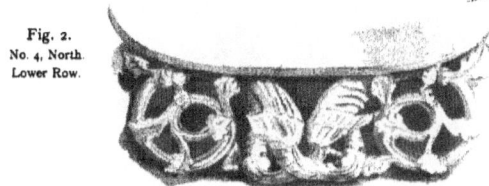

Fig. 3.
No 4, North

Plate 85.

Fig. 4.
Nó. 10, North
Lower Row

Fig. 5.
No. 1, North.
Lower Row.

Fig. 6.
No. 11, North.
Lower Row.

9. A demi-figure of a woman crouching, her fists clenched and held in front of her bosom. She wears a coif and the veil is extended behind her in a serpentine fashion.

10. A posture maker in long drapery, his jerkin showing below. He wears a hood with a long peak or liripipe, the end of which he seizes with his right hand, with his left he holds up his left foot behind.

Fig. 1. 11. A posture-maker with long hair, seated; his legs extend right and left, while he holds the feet on either side. The skirt of his tunic is cut in points.

12. A boar *couchant*.

13. A man lying on his side, his hood drawn over his head. He wears a jerkin bound round the waist with a belt, his legs crossed behind; his right arm is stretched out in front with the palm open, his left hand on his hip.

Fig. 7. 14. The demi-figure of a jovial little demon with open mouth, long pointed ears, fat cavy-like feet, and extended claws; behind his head is a cushion, tied at both ends, and covered with a foliated pattern.

15. A king crowned, clad in flowing drapery, lying in a crouching attitude on his side; his back supports the bracket.

16. A bat-faced demon with long claws, nails, and talons; its wings expanded.

17. A fox or wolf, cowled, lying with its head on a cushion similar to that in No. 14.

18. A jester putting the "apparel" of some ecclesiastical vestment round his neck.

North Side, commencing West: Lower Row.

Fig. 5. 1. A greyhound, stretched at full length, gnawing a bone.

2. A "Christchurch salmon," lying on rocks.

3. A jester in hood and laced-up jerkin, holding in his left hand a platter with a piece of bread on it, which a goose, swimming in water in the centre, is about to seize in its bill. In his right hand is the handle of some broken object (? a bauble).

Fig. 2. 4. Two dragons and foliage, their heads in base; no supporters. The carving is in full relief; it is thirteenth century work, and is said to be the oldest in England, though a misericord in Henry VII.'s Chapel claims a like honour.

5. A posture-maker in cap with long ears, going through contortions. On his left is some broken object, perhaps a snail.

6. An ape secured by a heavy chain and collar to the stump of a tree, in which is driven a ring-bolt.

7. A bat with wings extended at full length; below is fruit.

8. A rabbit warren; one rabbit running, while a second pops its head from one of the holes.

9. A large smooth face, winged like a cherub, but the wings are fastened together by two rings passed through them, joined by a link; below, on the right, appears a bird's nest.

Fig. 4 10. The emblem of St. Matthew. An angel, crowned and winged, seated, holding a long scroll in its hands. D. & S., human-headed bipeds.

Fig. 6 11. The emblem of St. Mark. A winged lion, holding a scroll in its paws. D. & S., *missing*.

The last two misericords were found lying loose in the Priory. They are fourteenth century.

South Side, commencing West : Lower Row.

1. A man in cap and flowing drapery, lying on his chest, and supporting the bracket with his left hand and right foot.

2. A demi-figure of a woman in a coif; wings spring from her shoulders.

Fig. 9 3. Demi-figure of a fat man, holding a scroll.

4. A vase full of berries or coins, from which hangs drapery on either side (very coarse).

5. A man in peasant's dress (the head gone), lying face downwards. (This misericord is upside down.)

6. A shield charged with a rose (County of Southampton), mantling, with a border behind (very coarse).

7. An embroidered chaplet *(broken)*.

8. An eagle with out-spread wings, holding a rosary in its beak.

9. A demi-figure of a man wearing a cap, his jerkin has puffed sleeves; his right arm is extended as if to throw something forward.

Fig. 8 10. Three crockets (boldly undercut). Fourteenth century.

11. *Missing.*

Fig. 7.
No. 14, North.

Fig. 8.
No. 10, South
Lower Row

Fig. 9.
No. 3, South.
Lower Row.

DURHAM CASTLE CHAPEL.

Twenty-two stalls remain, eleven of which have misericords. They were originally in Auckland Castle, having been placed there 1508—1522, in the time of Bishop Ruthall, whose arms appear on a bench end. They were removed to the Castle chapel in the time of Bishop Tunstall. The following entry appears in the accounts :—

> To Robert Champne, &c. 17 days in
> taking downe of the Stalls in the Highe
> Chapell and sortynge of them & dyght-
> inge of them and dresinge of them
> & helpinge to convey them to Durham   39s. viijd.

North Side, commencing West.

Fig. 2. 1. A man wheeling a woman in a wheel-barrow. She wields a scourge in her right hand, and clings to the barrow with her left. The man wears a short tunic and close-fitting cap. The barrow is constructed of two curved side-pieces which rest with their convexity on the ground when not in use. The wheel is a disc of wood cut out of the solid *(much broken)*. D. & S., rose.

Fig. 3. 2. A pig playing the bagpipes. Two young pigs and traces of a third are dancing to the music. D. & S., foliage.

3.
4. } *Missing.*

5. A unicorn with a long tail curled under its hind leg, and ending in three tufts across its haunch in most approved heraldic manner. D. & S., rose.

6. A man fighting a cockatrice or winged dragon; he thrusts a shield against its body. D., a mask. S., a mask with tongue protruding *(broken)*.

7. A mermaid, or child (her left arm broken off), holding in her right hand a comb (?). She issues from a whelk-shell, and a dragon turns back as if about to assail her. D. & S., foliage.

8. *Missing.* D. & S., roses.

9. A grotesque monster. D. & S., foliage with flowers.

10. *Missing.* D. & S., foliated ornament.

11. Foliage. D. & S., rose.

South Side, commencing West.

Fig. 1.   1. A man in civilian dress, mounted on horse-back, attacking a dragon with a spear. D. & S., flowers.

      2. A bear, muzzled and chained. D. & S., foliage.

         [The "supporters" appear to have been added at some time in place of the older ones, which were probably broken. The flat design is obtained by the simple process of lowering the ground round the outline.]

     3. } *Missing.*
     4. }

     5. Foliage. D. & S., rose.

     6. An eagle. D. & S., small eagle.

     7. }
     8. } *Missing.*
     9. }
     10. }

     11. An eagle-headed monster. D. & S., rose.

DURHAM CASTLE.

Plate 87.

Fig. 1.
No. 1, South.

Fig. 2.
No. 1, North

Fig. 3.
No. 2, North.

HENRY VII.'s CHAPEL, WESTMINSTER ABBEY.

The stalls are arranged in two rows on either side; those at the west end are of sixteenth century date (with the exception of one on the south side, which is thirteenth century), and are of fine design. Those at the east end are of Georgian production, and consist of two pieces. In the reign of George I. they were twice re-arranged. Two are returned, one on each side, and these two are of a larger size.

North Side, commencing West: Upper Row.

1. A man seated on a bench to the left, his hands clasped round his right knee. Opposite him is the figure of a woman (*broken*) lightly clad, and barefoot, raising her left foot. Behind her is another man, in a belted sleeved gown, wearing shoes; and on the extreme left is a man with a hat, pulling on his shoe. D. & S., large bunches of grapes.

Fig. 12.
2. A winged demon carrying off a monk on his back. The monk holds a bag in his hand, and his face is indicative of terror. D., a woman looking on in horror. S., a demon preceding the pair, beating a drum. [See No. 2, South Side, Upper Row.]

Fig. 2.
3. A man and woman seated. He has his arm round the woman's waist, and puts his hand into his gypcière, which hangs from his belt. The woman holds an empty purse in one hand, and with the other demands more money. Foliage at back. D., a dragon. S., a sow playing the flute.

    [The carving of this group is as rich in detail as a Dutch picture. The man, who may be a merchant or burgomaster, wears a fur cap and a handsome tunic; his gypcière is embroidered. The lady's dress is of satin-brocade, or some rich material, as is shown by the sharp folds, which are carefully reproduced.]

4. A man and woman, both nude but for hoods over their heads, opposite each other, discoursing music. D. & S., flower.

Fig. 1.
5. A magnificently-carved dragon. D., a wingless dragon. S., foliage on which a similar dragon stands, only the body remains. [See No. 5, South Side, Upper Row.]

6. An eagle with out-spread wings, on the top of a tree, to which it is fastened by chain and padlock. D., a lion. S., a dragon.

7. An ape seated on a stool, from which another seeks to displace him. To the right is another ape holding a rose. D., an ape astride a ram, with a three-thonged whip in his left hand. S., a man in a close hairy garment, with a twisted girdle, astride a horse, holding on by mane and tail.

8. *Broken.* D., an ape sitting on a windmill. S., an ape upsetting a flat basket (? winnowing basket) of wheat,

Fig. 5 9. The Judgment of Solomon ; so finely carved that the story can be read at a glance. The figures are, as usual, dressed in mediæval costume. The king is seated, crowned, on his throne, the dead child at his feet ; on either side the mothers kneel. The living child is held up, with scant ceremony, by a man who brandishes a sword over it. In the background are three courtiers ; one, dressed in a fur-lined robe like a lawyer, wears a cross round his neck—a whimsical anachronism ; another is apparently a monk, but his head is broken. D., a house, in the interior of which are the two women struggling over the living child, while the dead one lies in the foreground. S., a similar house, in which the mother and living child lie in bed. To them enters the other mother, holding her dead child in her arms ; she pulls back the clothes to change it.

[It is impossible, in the small size of the illustrations, to give an idea of the elaboration of the figures ; for instance, the woman and the child in bed have each a pillow with tassels at the corners. The women have the same dresses in the three scenes ; one has a cap, the other has her hair down.]

10. A semi-human monster with a club in his hand ; he grasps the tail of a dragon. D. & S., foliage.

Fig. 6. 11. A very plump mermaid, with a convex mirror, evidently made of polished steel or wood, on a stand with mouldings, in the latest fashion. D. & S., foliage.

12. A basket of foliage. D. & S., foliage.

13. A basket of flowers. D. & S., foliage.

14.
15.
16. Much inferior in design, and evidently later. The designs consist of flame-like foliage, with snake-like monsters therein.
17.
18.

South Side, commencing West : Upper Row.

1. A man and woman seated opposite each other. The man holds a child in his arms, the woman looks back at a child gathering grapes ; all are nude. The background is a delicately carved vine. D. & S., foliage. [Apparently a Bacchanalian group.]

Fig. 10. 2. A demon seizing a monk, who drops a money bag from which fall coins. The coins bear devices on them, one with a ship on it being apparently the "gold angel" ; the remainder are half-pennies of Henry VIII. [The episode here represented evidently precedes that depicted in No. 2, North Side.] D., demon with drum (*broken*.) S., cocks fighting (*broken*).

3. A man taking liberties with a woman who seizes him by the hair in self-defence. D. & S., fir-cones.

Fig. 14. 4. A bearded man, clad in a tunic with wide collar buttoned-up in front, placing his foot on the side of a lion and rending open its jaws ; he wears sandals and a turban. Trees in background. D., a lion and a lamb. S., a lion licking his hind leg, which is broken off.

5. A copy of No. 5, North Side. [A rare instance of such repetition. The centre dragon is not so sharply cut, and the sinister saurian is broken off in exactly the same place, as if the second carver did not know how such a beast should begin and end, and so resorted to this ingenious mode of escaping the difficulty.]

6. Foliage. D. & S., foliage with fruit.

Fig. 3. 7. A wodehouse with scaly limbs, clad in a buttoned, sleeveless jacket, fighting a cockatrice with a club; the monster has hold of his right ankle. Behind the man is another monster, which bites his right elbow, and seizes his left ankle. In the foreground two snakes come out of holes, and another snake peeps from the branches above. In the background stands a tree, in which is a nest containing three eggs. It may be some enchanted forest, with the creatures guarding the nest. D., a man in a tunic, holding up a horse-shoe to three ostriches. S., a man in a tunic, with side-laced boots, astride a lion, tearing its jaws open.

8. A bearded man, nude, wrestling with a bear. D. & S., fir-cones.

Fig. 8. 9. Foliage.

N.B.—This foliage is thirteenth century work and claims, like one at Christchurch, to be the oldest in England.

10. A lion, *couchant gardant*. D. & S., foliage.

11. A curly-headed boy, holding the head of another between his knees, while a third lays on with a birch rod. D. & S., foliage.

12. Two monsters. D. & S., foliage.

13. A head in foliage. D. & S., foliage.

14. ⎫
15. ⎪
16. ⎬ Inferior, as in Upper Row, N.
Fig. 15. 17. ⎪
18. ⎭

North Side, commencing West; Lower Row.

1. Two wodehouses, the one on the left has a long sword. D. & S., foliage.

2. *Query*, Goliath and David. A castle gate open with the portcullis drawn up. In the gateway a man and woman come out *(heads gone)*. The man wears a mantle and a gypcière depends from his girdle. To the right a man with a spear meets them. A small figure, in tunic with gypcière is at the gate; behind him, a gigantic headless figure with a spear at his side. There is a rabbit warren with three rabbits in it. D., a giant armed with a spear and sword, advancing against a small figure preparing to sling a stone at him. Behind, stands a castle with three figures, one a woman, looking over the walls. S., a giant with his left hand over the walls of a castle; in his right a staff or spear.

Fig. 9. 3. A head in foliage. D. & S., foliage.

4. A shield, charged quaterly, France and England, surmounted by a crown. The supporters are griffins. D. & S., foliage.

N

Fig. 7.
5.
6. } Foliage. D. & S., foliage.
7.

8. Two boys seated, one with a cap on, with his right hand on the branch of a tree ; the other bare-headed with his hands on his knees. D. & S., foliage.

9.
10.
11. } *Modern.*
12.
13.

Fig. 13. 14. A phœnix. D. & S., dragon and snake.

15.
16. } *Modern.*

South Side, commencing West : Lower Row.

1. A woman in a hood standing over a prostrate man, chastising him with a distaff. He attempts to save his head from her blows. D., A jester in cap with cockscomb. S., a man putting his tongue out, extending his mouth with his fingers.

2. A woman in a hood, beating a man with a birch as he kneels before her. He holds a ball of yarn in his right hand and a winding-frame in his left. D. & S., foliage.

3. A man in a loose coat seated with his arm round a woman's waist, apparently laying his hand on her knee (*broken*). She holds the branch of a tree with her right hand and pushes him away with her left. D., a boy, nude, in foliage. S., a lad with a birch in his hand.

4. Two wodehouses, fighting. One kneels and shoots with a bow at the other, who cowers behind a curved shield. D. & S., foliage, with fir-cones.

Fig. 11. 5. Two small, chubby-faced boys playing "cocklety bread." D., a boy with shield and staff. S., a boy astride a cock-horse.

6. Two grotesque monsters fighting. D. & S., foliage and flowers.

Fig. 4. 7. Apes with young ones. One has fruit in his hands, the other a young one in her lap. another baby sits by her (*head missing*). D., a bear with collar and chain playing the bagpipes. S., a monkey seated on a block to which he is chained, holding up a bottle.

8.
9.
10.
11. } *Modern.*
12.
13.
14.
15.
16. A hydra.

Fig. 10.
No. 2, South

Fig. 11.
No. 5, South
Lower Row

Fig. 12.
No. 2, North

Fig. 13.
No. 14, North
Lower Row.

Fig. 14.
No. 4, South.

Fig. 15.
No. 17, South.

BEVERLEY MINSTER, YORKSHIRE.

The sixty-eight choir stalls were placed in the Minster in 1520, about thirty years before the dissolution of the collegiate establishment, as is shown by the date carved on one of them. Some of them bear the arms of members of the Collegiate Society. One of the finest series of misericords in England. The front of the brackets is enriched with a row of small arches; the "supporters" are encircled by the bracket moulding, fastened with a foliated clasp.

North Side, commencing West.

1. A stag chased by hounds, passing to the right. A man clothed in a tight jerkin runs up and pierces it with a spear; his hounds wear spiked collars. Below, a rabbit pops its head out of its burrow. D., a man riding a caparisoned horse to the right, winding a horn. S., a doe scratching her head with her hind hoof.
2. A man standing in the centre, piercing a lion through the head with a spear. His left hand and the shaft of the spear are broken. D., a lion *passant regardant.* S., a lion *passant*, with tongue protruding.
3. A unicorn, *passant regardant.* D. & S., foliage.
4. A fox in a hood, in a pulpit, holding a rosary, preaching to seven geese. Behind him stands an ape as clerk with a goose slung over a pole on his back. In the back-ground a fox runs to the right with a goose in its mouth. The "satirical rogue" of a carver has represented the goose on the back row indulging in a quiet nap, during the homily. D., an owl with wings extended. S., a man shoeing a goose. [A repetition of the one at Whalley.]
5. A man dressed in a short tunic, a gypcière hanging from his belt, holding a hawk on his left wrist. His attendant, holding two hounds in leash, runs to the right. The attendant, besides a gypcière, has a dagger. D., a cock facing to the right. S., a dog gnawing a bone. Two scrolls, one round each "supporter" bear the inscriptions, **Johannis Syerhe Clericus Fabrici.**
6. A tree in centre, on either side a hart and a doe, browsing. D., a hart leaping to the left. S., a doe and her fawn.
7. A fox hanged by six geese, who hold the rope in their beaks. To the right are two fowls, which are armed respectively with sword and mace. D., a fox prowling near two sleepy fowls. S., an ape removing the fatal noose from his friend's neck, after the execution.
8. A mask with protruding tongue, foliage issues from the mouth. D., a man chopping a branch from a tree. S., foliage.

Fig. 3. (beside item 3)
Fig. 2 (beside item 4)
Fig. 1. (beside item 7)

9. Two monsters fighting, the left one is human-headed. D., a dog-faced baboon grasping a pole. S., a creature with long tail and indented back crouching, looking back and opening his mouth.

10. A man dressed in a tunic with a belt, warming his hands at a fire. In the centre a woman (*broken*) chases a dog which has stolen a piece of meat from the "stand pot" and runs away to the right. D., a scullion kneeling before a pot, washing platters; one dish hangs over his head. He wears an apron over his short tunic. S., a man pulling up his hose. His shoes lie on the ground and his wallet is hung up on the wall.

Fig. 12. 11. A man dressed in short tunic (his head gone), mounted on a horse passing to the right. In his right hand he bears a staff or fork (*broken*). At the side stands a cart, now called a harvest cart, with open sides and two large wheels. D., a cow lying down, licking itself. S., a maid milking a cow, with a pail with three hoops. A pretty group.

12. A shield supported on the dexter side by a hawk, on the sinister by a hound. The shield is charged, on a fess the rays of the sun between three birds, two and one. D., a bird, below which is a scroll, inscribed 𝕬𝖗𝖒𝖆 𝖂𝖎𝖑𝖍𝖊𝖑𝖒𝖎 𝕮𝖆𝖎𝖙 𝕯𝖔𝖈𝖙𝖔𝖗𝖊𝖘. S., a hawk with wings expanded, above which is a scroll, inscribed 𝕿𝖍𝖊𝖘𝖆𝖚𝖗𝖎𝖎 𝕳𝖚𝖏𝖚𝖘 𝕰𝖈𝖈𝖑𝖎𝖊, 𝟏𝟓𝟐𝟎.

Fig. 11. 13. In the centre a man turned to the left, thrusting with both hands a spear into the mouth of a boar which attacks him. His hound seizes another boar by the ear. He is clad in a short *cote hardi* and wears a round cap, flat at the top. D. & S., a circular flower.

14. A wodehouse with long hair, kneeling on his right knee fighting a dragon. He carries a shield on his left arm and raises a falchion in his right hand. D. & S., fruit.

15. The bust of a man grimacing. He wears a tight-fitting cap with brim turned up at the sides. His elbows are raised on a level with the top of his head, and with his fingers he distends the corners of his mouth. D. & S., lion's mask with tongue protruding.

16. A cock with extended wings, facing to the left. D., a cock pluming himself. S., two cocks fighting, perched on a barrel.

Fig. 8. 17. A man wheeling a woman in a barrow. She wears a kerchief on her head and her dress is full at the neck. With her right hand she grasps the side of the barrow and with her left she seizes the man's hair. (His right arm and the right handle of the barrow are gone.) D., a man lifting a beam of wood. S., a woman catching a dog by the neck.

18. A woman standing in the centre. Her right hand is on the "stand-pot," from which a dog is helping himself; with her left she seizes a man by the hair. She wears a kerchief on her head. D., a woman grinding a hand-mill, a bag hangs on the wall before her. S., a man chopping a billet of wood.

[For once, let imagination have free scope in explaining the episode which inspired the three examples, 10, 17, and 18. During one of those domestic

Fig. 1.
No. 5, North

Fig. 2.
No. 3, North.

Fig. 3.
No. 7. South.

Plate 89.

Fig. 4.
No. 7, South
Lower Row

Fig. 5.
No. 9, North

Fig. 6.
No. 11, North.

Fig. 7.
No. 6, North.
Lower Row.

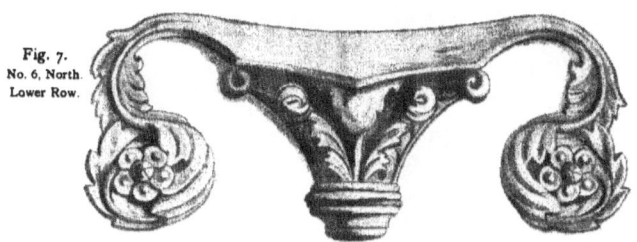

Fig. 8.
No. 9, South

Fig. 9.
No. 3, North
Lower Row

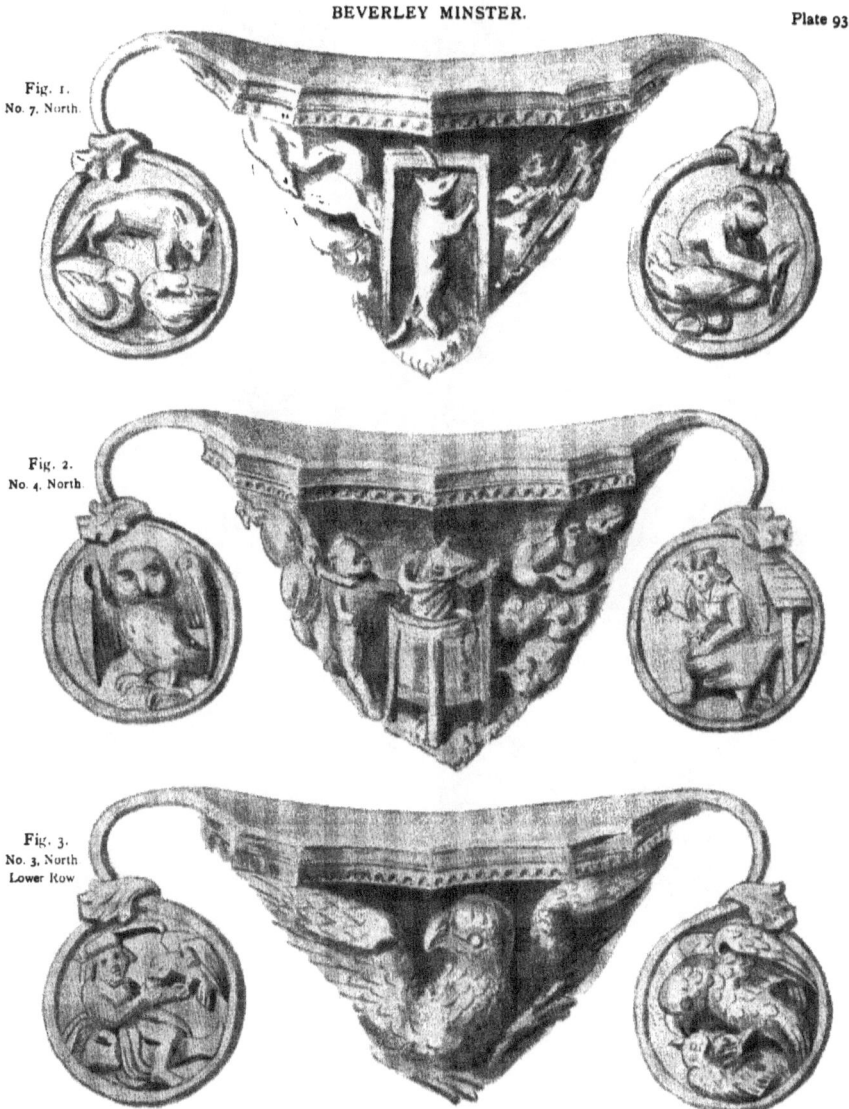

Fig. 1.
No. 7. North.

Fig. 2.
No. 4. North.

Fig. 3.
No. 3, North
Lower Row

Fig. 4.
No. 3, North

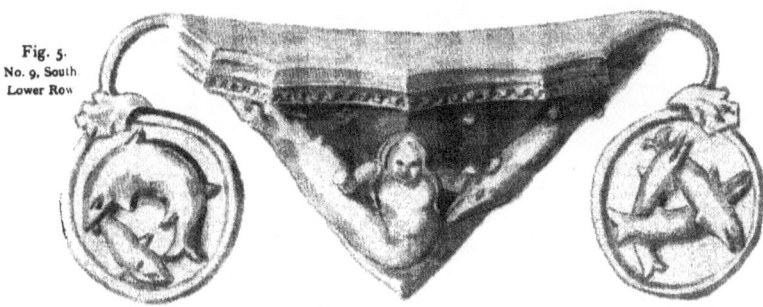

Fig. 5.
No. 9, South
Lower Row

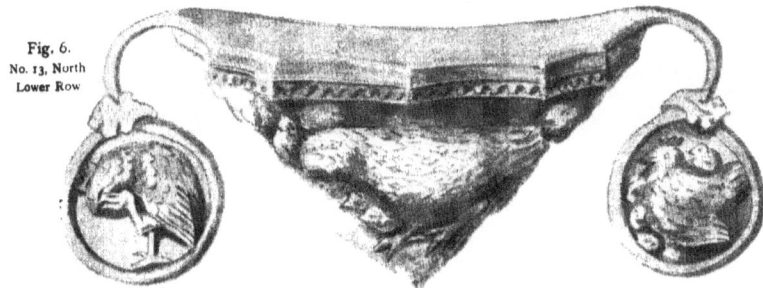

Fig. 6.
No. 13, North
Lower Row

disturbances, which seem to have been rather frequent, a dog has entered the kitchen and made free with the contents of the pot in front of the fire; the housewife, indignant at the dog's theft, has captured him, and has relieved her feelings by chastising him; or, it may be, by consigning him to a watery grave. Her husband, who is at work in the yard, hears the cries of his favourite for help, and comes, perhaps too late, to save him; exasperated by the outrage, caused by the ill-temper which his wife's face displays, he revenges himself by wheeling her off to the nearest horse-pond.—E.P.]

19. A dragon-headed bird with human face on its breast. D. & S., small dragon.

20. A demi-angel, *volant*, in an alb, its wings extended, and its hands raised high on either side. D., a bunch of grapes and vine leaves. S., a rose on a spray of leaves.

21. Three jesters, hand-in-hand, dancing; they wear hoods with long ears, and their tunics are scalloped. D., a jester kneeling, his right hand raised as if instructing an audience, his left hand holds a staff and bladder. S., a jester playing the fife and tabor.

South Side, commencing West: Upper Row.

1. A pelican *in her piety*; the nest contains six young. D., a pelican standing with out-spread wings. S., a pelican turned to the left, pecking its left claw.

2. An ape riding a horse, face to the tail, holding on to its mane with its left hand; the horse is going to the left. Behind, to the right, is a man who raises a club to smite the ape; the man's arms are broken off. D., an ape mounted on a cat going to the right, which he combs with a large comb. S., a boy mounted on a pig, running to the left; he holds the pig's tail in his right hand.

3. A demi-angel in an alb, with extended wings, bearing in front the Sacred Heart. D. & S., fruit and foliage.

4. A shield, charged: a fess between two weights, two and one. The scroll round the shield bears the inscription 𝔚𝔦𝔩𝔩𝔦𝔪 𝔚𝔶𝔫𝔥𝔱 𝔗𝔢𝔪𝔭𝔬𝔯𝔢 𝔠𝔞𝔫𝔠𝔢𝔩𝔩𝔞𝔯𝔦𝔰 𝔥𝔲𝔦𝔲𝔰 𝔈𝔠𝔠𝔩𝔢𝔯𝔦𝔢. D., a man bearing a weight in each hand. S., a man holding a pair of scales which hang from the moulding, raising his left foot from the ground.

5. A lion fighting a dragon. D., a baboon seated, facing to the right, holding up an infant in swathing bands. S., a baboon seated, facing to the left, holding up a bottle.

6. A pedlar lying asleep, in the foreground; his head to the right. Behind his head is his pack, which eight apes ransack. One ape on the right is gazing into a circular mirror, another to the left is passing out the articles to his fellows. D., an ape seated on a leaf, grasping the moulding with his left hand, holding out his right hand for a share of the spoil. S., a cat in a tree; below which, facing to the right, is an ape with a staff in his hand. These two seats resemble two at Manchester.

7. A shield, behind which is a scroll, charged : a fess, between three weights, two and one. D., a man with hood and liripipe, raising two weights from the ground. S., a man walking to the left, carrying two weights.

8. Foliage. D. & S., leaves.

9. A woman standing in the centre (the upper part of her body is broken off). To the right a man in a cap kneels and blows a fire with bellows ; to the left, a man chopping wood with an axe. D. & S., fruit and foliage.

10. Two men dragging a wicker cage in which lies a bear. In the centre stands a man holding in both hands a staff. D., a man, facing to the left, putting a muzzle on a bear which crouches at his feet. S., a man muzzling a bear which stands on its hind legs and grasps him by the left leg.

11. A man in a cap seated in the centre, holding a sheep under his left arm, his hands being clasped in front of him. Behind the trunk of a tree (?) to the right a ram, and behind that again, another ; to the left, a man astride a ram which he holds by the tail, and shears ; three shorn sheep stand behind him. D., a shepherd passing to the left, a crook in his left hand ; he strokes his dog with the right. S., two rams butting in front of a tree.

12. A shield, supported on either side by a griffin, charged : quaterly, 1 and 4, three billets, in chief, three balls ; 2 and 3, a chevron between three mullets, two and one. D., a pelican *in her piety* below a scroll bearing, 𝕬𝖗𝖒𝖆 𝕸𝖆𝖌𝖎𝖘𝖙𝖗𝖎 𝕿𝖍𝖔𝖒𝖊. S., a doe facing to the left, collared and chained, lying on a tun (?). Behind the doe is a scroll bearing 𝕯𝖔𝖓𝖞𝖓𝖆𝖙𝖔' 𝖄' 𝖈𝖊𝖓𝖙𝖔𝖗𝖎𝖘 𝕼𝖚𝖎𝖘 𝕰𝖈𝖈𝖑𝖎𝖊.

13. Two men hauling a rope attached to a muzzled bear ; from the left a man wheels a barrow to receive the beast. D., a man, facing left, grasping a dog's muzzle with his left hand, while with his right hand he endeavours to thrust the dog's head from under the lappet of his coat ; the animal, no doubt, scents game. S., a muzzled bear licking its paw.

14. A dead stag, lying on its back, being cut up by two men ; one behind the centre of its body gives directions to the second, who stands between its hind legs ; a dog lies on either side. D., a man holding a hound in leash. S., a man, facing to the right, winding a horn ; he is surrounded by five baying hounds.

15. A bear (?) attacked by four hounds, one on his back biting his left ear, one on the right, and one in front ; a fourth, badly hurt, under him. To the right are two men, one running with a staff in his hand, the other winds a horn. D., a man holding up a three-thonged whip over an ape which cowers in front of him and raises its hands in supplication. S., a monkey seated, facing to the right, playing the bagpipes to a muzzled bear, which dances before him.

16. An ape seated on a horse, which drags three muzzled bears to the left by a chain ; a dog precedes him. D., a bear muzzled. S., a man facing to the right, holding a dog by its hind-quarter and biting its tail.

Plate 95.

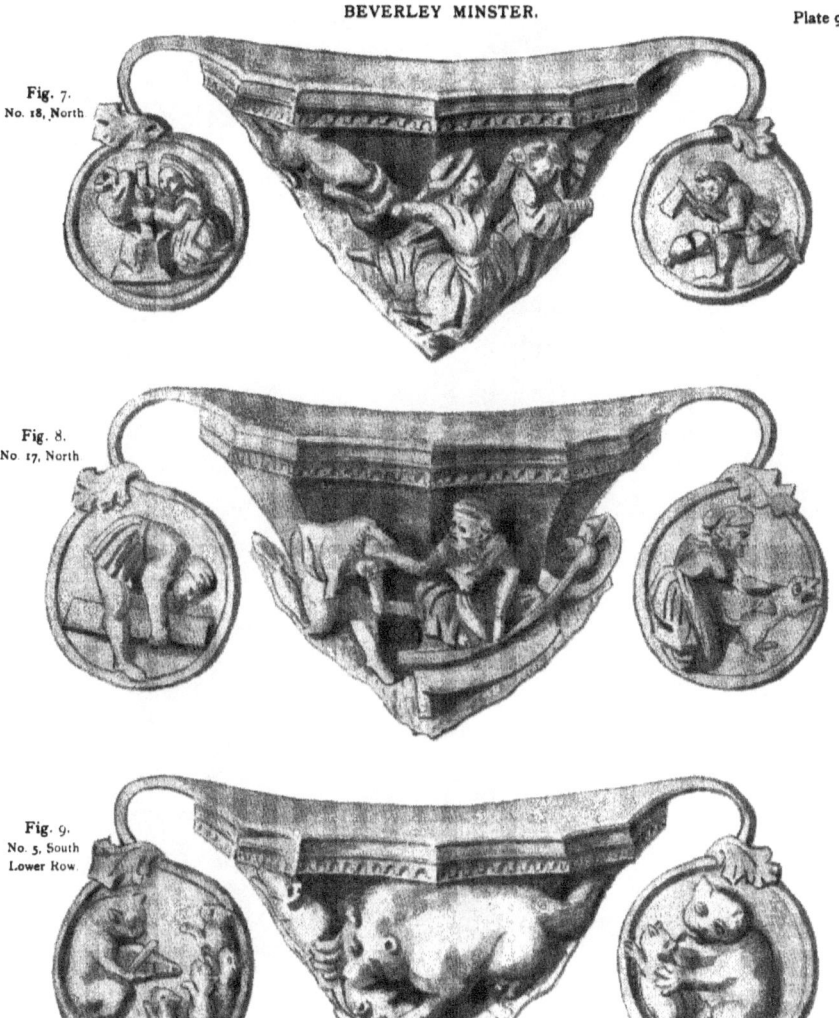

Fig. 7.
No. 18, North

Fig. 8.
No. 17, North

Fig. 9.
No. 5, South
Lower Row.

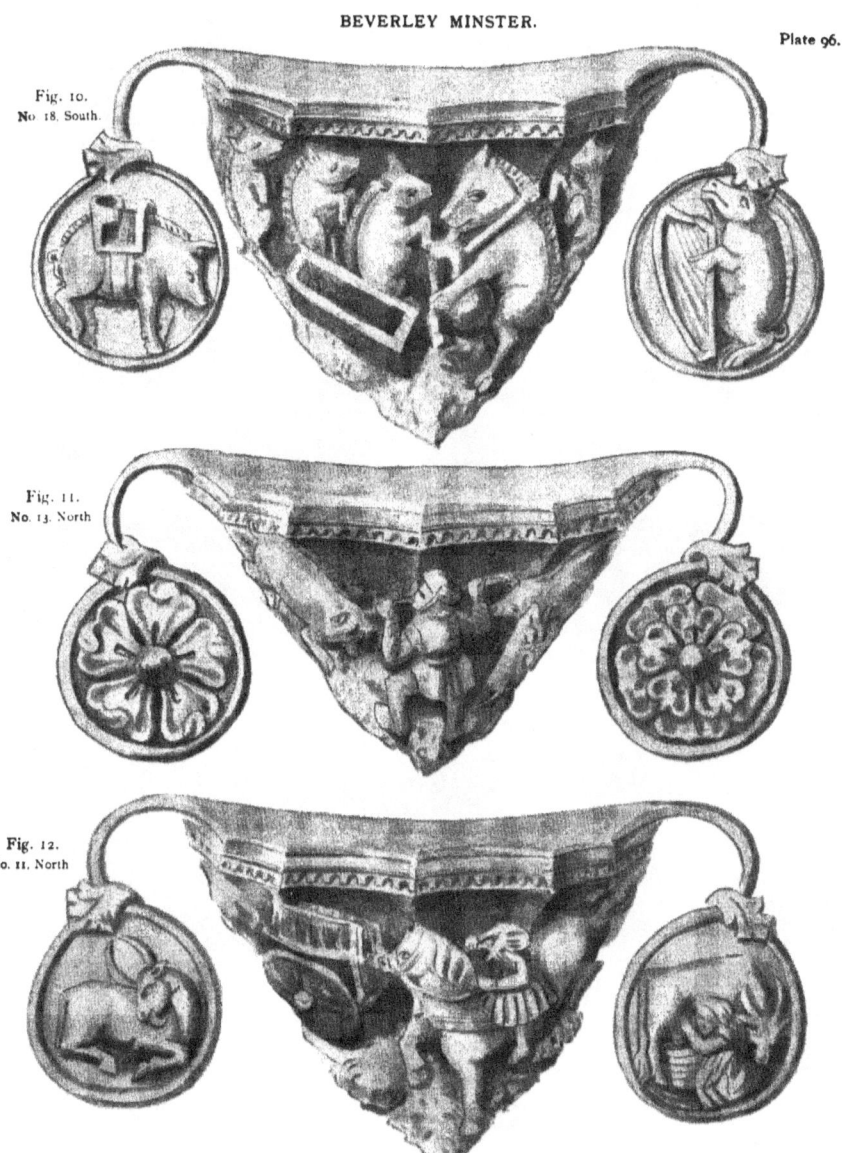

Fig. 10.
No 18, South.

Fig. 11.
No. 13, North

Fig. 12.
No. 11, North

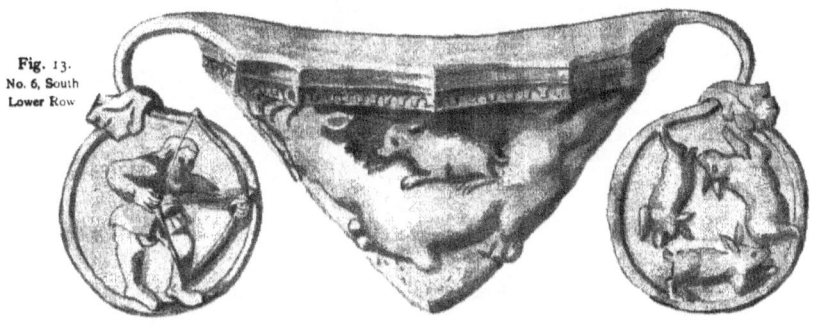

Fig. 13.
No. 6, South
Lower Row

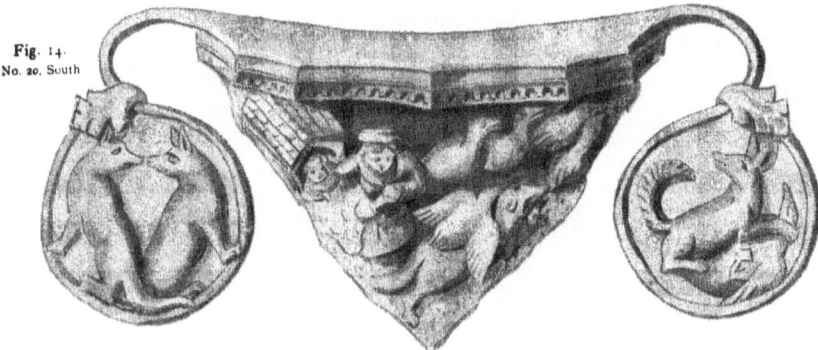

Fig. 14.
No. 20, South

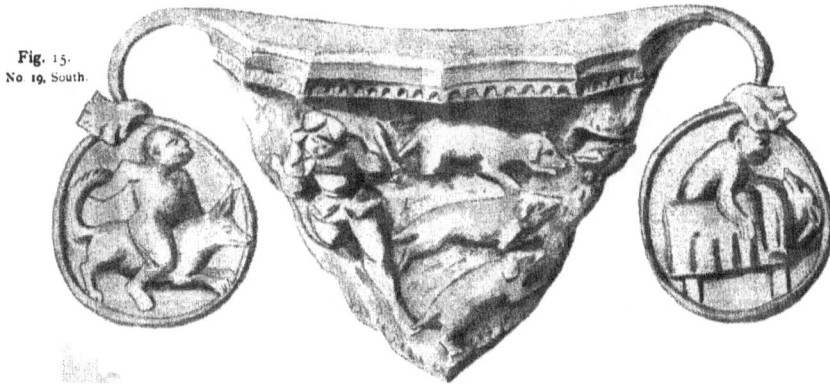

Fig. 15.
No 19, South.

17. A man in a cap, fighting two dragons, whose tails wind round his body. He thrusts his right hand into the mouth of the left, and has been holding a weapon in his other hand, but it is broken off. D., a man in a hooded cape, spearing a snail. S., a man creeping into a sack.

Fig. 10. 18. A sow standing on her hind legs to the right, playing the bagpipes. A trough in front ; four young pigs dance. D., a saddled pig. S., a pig standing on its hind legs, playing the harp.

Fig. 15. 19. Three hounds running in front of a man, who bears a bow and arrow (*broken*). A fox thrusts its head out from its earth. D., an ape riding on a fox. S., an ape nursing, or shriving, a fox, which lies in bed.

Fig. 14. 20. A fox running away with a goose ; behind him the good-wife gives chase. To the left is the farm-house with the child standing in the doorway. Behind the fox are four geese. D., two foxes seated facing each other, in consultation. S., a fox looking back over its shoulder ; a goose under its paws.

21. Grapes and foliage. D. & S., bunches of grapes and vine leaves.

North Side, commencing West: Lower Row.

1. Two lions seated, *counter regardant ;* the sinister is crowned. D., a boar, *passant.* S., a hawk, *regardant.*

2. Two men fighting, the right hand man is clothed and bears a shield of peculiar shape, on which is a face ; he raises a sword (*broken*) in his right hand to strike his opponent ; the scabbard hangs on his right side. The man on the left is nude ; he raises his right hand to stab the clothed man with a dagger. D. & S., leaves.

Fig. 3. 3. A hawk with out-spread wings. D., a man seated, holding a hawk on his wrist and feeding it with his right hand. S., a hawk preying on a pigeon. [The custodian informs visitors that the D. "supporter" represents Elijah fed by the ravens, and adds "And I don't think much of Elijah." Certainly it would be difficult to imagine anything less like a dignified Eastern seer than the jaunty figure of the falconer.]

4. A rose tree bearing four Tudor roses. D. & S., Tudor rose.

5. A hawk or cock flying after a bat. D., a bird scratching its head. S., a cock doing the same.

6. A lion facing to the right, placing his right paw on a prostrate man's head. D., a wyvern with out-spread wings. S., a griffin.

7. Two geese standing on the head of a jester and pecking his hood which has long ears. D., a goose pluming itself. S., a swan *naiant.*

8. Large bust of a jester, wearing a hood with long ears, putting the right forefinger in his mouth, the left hand over his left eye. D., a goose flying. S., a goose pluming itself.

9. An owl attacked by four small birds. D. & S., bird with wings extended.

10. Two dragons flying away from each other. D., a raven perched on a branch. S., a dove perched on foliage.

11. The large bust of a jester in an eared hood ; he is grinning and showing his teeth. D., a clean shaven face, laughing. S., a hooded head, with the mouth puckered up, perhaps whistling.

12. Foliage. D. & S., leaves.

Fig. 6   13. A hen with five chickens. D., a cock scratching his comb. S., a hen sitting on her chickens. Three pretty, well-carved groups.

South Side, commencing West: Lower Row.

1. A demon armed with a mace with spikes, running to the left after a woman, whose head and hands are broken off. The imp has a human face on his breast and a long tail hangs behind ; he stretches forward his left hand to seize her. D., a man hooded, seated before a money-chest, counting his hoard ; the head of a demon peeps over at him. S., a fat-paunched man seated, drinking out of a bottle which he holds in his right hand. In his left he holds some object like a leg of mutton, or a ham. A demon reaches up towards him with his left arm. The " supporters " no doubt represent avarice and gluttony, and the figure chased is a lost soul.

2. Foliage. D. & S., flowers and leaves.

3. An owl with out-spread wings, holding a mouse in its claw. D. & S., leaves.

4. Two cranes pecking corn out of a sack. Their wings are out-spread. D. & S., cranes with out-spread wings.

Fig. 9.   5. A cat seizing a mouse in her right claw ; with her left paw, with sheathed talons, she encourages her kitten to give chase. D., a cat playing the viol to four kittens, who dance. S., a cat playing with her kitten.

Fig. 13.   6. A rabbit riding on an animal, probably a fox, guiding it by a rope held in the mouth of the two animals. D., a man drawing a long bow, holding one end with his foot. S., three rabbits running round in a circle.

7. Lion and antelope, *couchant counter regardant.* D., a lion crowned, *couchant.* S., an antelope or unicorn scratching its head with its hind hoof.

8. Two demi-figures of carvers ; they wear tight jerkins. The one on the right places his left hand on the other's left shoulder and raises a mallet to strike. The other holds a chisel in his left hand and tries to escape. D., a man putting his left hand to his nose : he wears a cap. S., a man in a flat cap, and belt round his waist, is raising his hands in wonder.

Fig. 5.   9. A mermaid, her arms broken off at the elbows ; at her left side swims a dolphin. There are marks on the bracket where she has held two objects. D., a large fish swallowing a smaller one. S., three fishes interlaced in a triangle.

10. Foliage. D. & S., foliage.

11. Joshua and Caleb, the two spies, carrying a large bunch of grapes on a pole, a dog in front of them. D. & S., bunches of grapes and leaves.

12. Two lions, *couchant counter gardant.* D. & S., square foliated ornament.

13. An elephant passing to the left, a large castle on his back ; his ears are webbed like a bat's. Behind, an ape urges him on with a staff ; a porcupine leads the way. D., a camel, *couchant.* S., a lion, *gardant.*

KING'S COLLEGE, CAMBRIDGE.

The woodwork of the choir of the chapel was completed in the
reign of Henry VIII., 1534. It shows, as Mr. T. J. P. Carter observes,
" that the Gothic epoch in the history of the chapel is at an end ;
" that the rude energy of the Northern conquerors has given place to
" the refinement of the South ; and that Italian wood carvers and
" Flemish draughtsmen tread in the steps of the English freemasons."

There are one hundred and eighteen stalls with misericords,
eight of which are returned. The returned stalls and two on each
side are Renaissance in style, and bear graceful scrolls in very low
relief ; they differ in their mode of ornamentation from all other
seats. The rest of the misericords are of a different date ; the
ornament is a head or foliage supporting the bracket, without
" supporters."

WIMBORNE MINSTER, DORSET.

There were originally eighteen stalls in the fine Minster, but only fourteen survive. None are returned of the seven on each side of the choir. They are all foliage, the bracket being particularly heavy. They were the gift of the Bankers family, and are well known as Jacobean, dating 1608.

WIMBORNE MINSTER.

Plate 100.

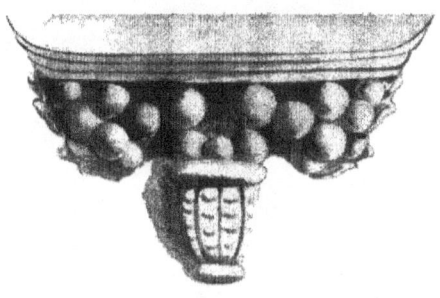

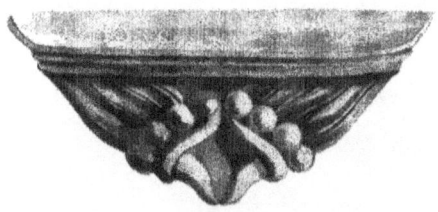

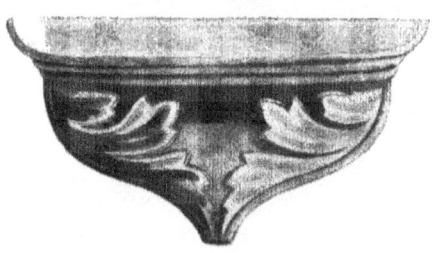

Plate 101.

DURHAM CATHEDRAL.

Fig. 1.
No 14, South

Fig. 2.
No 7, South

Fig. 3.
No 10, North

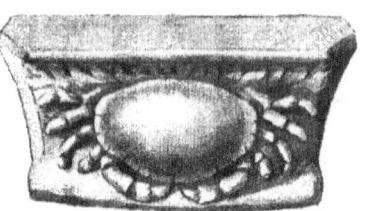

DURHAM CATHEDRAL.

There are thirty-two stalls, six on each side having been destroyed. They are very late in date, erected by Bishop Cosin (1660-1663). Four are returned. There are no "supporters."

North Side, commencing West.

1. An eagle.
2. A winged monster. The head is that of an eagle, the body that of a lion, with serpent's tail ending in a large sting.
3. A similar monster.
4. A monster like a wolf.
5. Figure of a boy ending in foliage, on each side of him a cornucopia.
6. A figure of a child issuing from foliage, the base of which terminates in an eagle's head.
7. A foliated figure, with her hand to her mouth. Foliage round.
8. An ape with an apple.
9. A squirrel with a nut.

Fig. 3. 10. A crab.
11. A peacock with tail out-spread.
12. A female figure with cornucopia.
13. A peacock with tail out-spread.
14. A mermaid between two dolphins.
15. A lion with large mane, its ribs very prominent.
16. A shield of oval form uncharged, supported by two lions.

South Side, commencing West.

1. A lion, *coward passant.*
2. A demi-figure of a man issuing from foliage, blowing a conch-shell.
3. A horse lying down.
4. A monster, to whose open mouth some round object is offered by a man.
5. A winged boy, surrounded by foliage and fruit.
6. A human-headed monster, and a dragon.

Fig. 2. 7. A human-headed foliated monster with foliage.
8. A boy with fruit.
9. A mermaid and dolphins.
10. A squirrel with a nut.
11. A merman and mermaid.
12. A boy issuing from foliage ; cornucopias.
13. Squirrel with a nut and fir-cones.

Fig. 1. 14. A fish-like monster on a dolphin.
15. A child pursued by a lion.
16. An oval shield supported by two lions.

ALPHABETICAL LIST OF SUBJECTS

AND OF

THE PLACES WHERE THEY OCCUR,

ARRANGED, AS FAR AS POSSIBLE, IN CHRONOLOGICAL ORDER.

ABRAHAM SACRIFICING ISAAC. Worcester.

ABSALOM. Gayton.

ADAM AND EVE. Ely; Worcester; Chester; Bristol.

ADORATION OF THE MAGI. Lincoln.

ALEWIFE. Ely; Wellingborough; All Souls', Oxford; Fairford; Ludlow.

AMICE. An oblong piece of linen with an embroidered portion at one end; this is sometimes worn round the neck like a collar, and sometimes drawn over the head like a hood. It was worn by all the clergy above the four minor orders. Ludlow; Manchester.

ANGEL HOLDING HEART. Emblem of St. Augustine, St. Theresa.

APES. Chichester; Ely; Lincoln; Lancaster; Sherborne; Ripon; Bedford; Christchurch; St. Andrew's, Norwich; Magdalen College; Westminster Abbey.

APE AND MONKS. St. Mary's, Beverley.

  ,, WITH BOTTLE. Cartmel; Faversham; Boston; Beverley.

  ,, ON CAT. Beverley.

  ,, NURSING DOLL OR BABY. Manchester; Beverley.

  ,, ON HORSEBACK. Beverley.

  ,, ON RAM. Westminster Abbey.

  ,, WHEELING ANOTHER IN BARROW. Norwich.

  ,, APES AND PEDLAR. An incident taken from the story of Reynard the Fox. Manchester; Bristol; Beverley; Windsor.

APPAREL. A small embroidered piece of linen sewn on the albe, the amice, and other ecclesiastical vestments. Christchurch.

ARBALEST. A name given to the cross-bow used by soldiers. It was frequently of such large size that the bow required to be drawn by an iron wheel; the bow being held firm by the foot placed in a stirrup in the centre. The wheel, when not in use, was carried at the soldier's girdle. Bedford.

- ARIES. The sign of the Zodiac for March. Beverley.

ARK (see Noah).

ASCENSION, THE. Lincoln.

ASS. The emblem of patience, also of stubbornness and stupidity. Gloucester.

,, AND WOODMAN. Bristol.

,, AND CAT. Hereford.

BACKGAMMON, OR TRIC-TRAC. Windsor; Manchester.

BALL-PLAYING. Gloucester.

BANASTER (ARMS). Passenham.

BASILISK. The emblem of the Spirit of Evil. The glance of the basilisk caused death, so it could only be conquered by holding a mirror or polished shield before it, when it died of fright at its own image. Worcester; Malvern; Faversham; Ludlow; Manchester.

BEAR. Gloucester; Durham Castle.

,, AND FOX. Bristol.

,, IN BARROW. Beverley.

,, DANCING. Bristol.

,, BAITING. Boston; St. Mary's, Beverley; Manchester.

,, PLAYING ORGAN. Boston.

,, PLAYING BAGPIPES. Boston.

,, BEATING DRUM. Boston.

BEAUCHAMP (ARMS). Leighton Buzzard.

BEAVER. Worcester; Windsor.

BISHOP. Beddington; All Souls'; Ludlow; St. Margaret's, Lynn.

BLIND MAN'S BUFF. Bristol.

- BOAR. In the large forests herds of boars still ranged. September was the month for hunting them. The presence of a row of stiff bristles down the back of carved specimens shows that domestic swine were not far removed from their wild progenitors.

BOVILLE (ARMS). Norwich.

BULL. The emblem of St. Luke. Bampton; Fordham; Passenham.

BUTCHER KILLING OX. Worcester; Malvern.

CAMEL. Emblem of endurance. Boston; Manchester.

CANTERBURY (ARMS). Maidstone.

CARVER AT WORK. Wellingborough; Brampton; St. Nicholas, Lynn; Christchurch.

CARVERS QUARRELLING. Beverley.

CASTLE. The badge of Edward II., for Castile. Bedford; New College, Oxford.

CAT AND ASS. Hereford.

CAT AND FOX. Bristol.

  ,, AND KITTENS. Beverley.

  ,, HANGED BY RATS. Malvern.

CENTAUR. Exeter; Chichester; Lincoln; Ely; New College.

CHARITY (?). Gayton.

CHERUB. King's College.

CHICHELE (ARMS). Higham Ferrers.

CHILD OR MERMAID emerging from a shell, fighting a dragon, signifies purity conquering sin. Worcester; Lincoln; Chester; Manchester; Durham Castle.

CITHERN. A musical instrument something like a guitar. It was at one time placed in every barber's shop, to beguile the time of waiting. The instrument generally had a grotesque head carved on it. Minster; St. Mary's, Beverley.

CIRCUMCISION. Worcester.

COCK. A Welsh badge. Symbol of courage and watchfulness, being always ready armed for battle. With St. Peter it signified repentance, and in this sense was one of the emblems of the Passion. Beverley; Westminster.

COCK RIDING FOX. Westminster.

COLUMBINE. A badge of Henry IV. Manchester.

COOK AND UTENSILS, Minster; Windsor; Maidstone.

COSIN'S EAGLE. Durham Castle.

COURTENAY (ARMS). Maidstone.

COWL OR CAPUCHON. Was worn by all classes till Henry VIII. prohibited its use by persons below the rank of esquire in the royal household.

CRAB. Durham Cathedral.

CRANE. Lincoln.

CROWD OR VIOL. A fiddle, a popular musical instrument. Chichester; Ely.

CROWN. Hemington; Cartmel; Gayton.

DAVID AND GOLIATH. Westminster.

DEATH CLAIMING BOTH KING AND "HODGE." Windsor.

DEER. Signifies sometimes solitude and purity of life, and sometimes baptism. It is the attribute of St. Julian Hospitaller. When it has a crucifix between its horns it refers to the legend of St. Hubert. Of frequent occurrence.

  ,, HERALDIC. The badge of Richard II. and Edward IV.; chained, Henry VI. As the stag was borne by many families, it is probable that patrons of the various churches were thus represented. Minster; Ripon; Beverley; Ludlow; Manchester.

DEMON. The mediæval devil is a being who takes the keenest delight in his evil work of temptation and punishment. His introduction afforded the carver full scope for his love of grotesque humour. He is represented in a variety of forms: with and without wings and a tail, with claws and human feet; in fact, the main object seems to have been to make him at the same time repulsive and amusing. Occurs everywhere.

DEMON CHASING A LOST SOUL. Beverley.

  ,,   CARRYING OFF MONK. Westminster.

  ,,   CARRYING OFF ALEWIFE. Ludlow.

  ,,   CARRYING OFF MAN. Faversham.

  ,,   AND NUNS. Ely; St. Katharine's Hospital.

  ,,   DRAWING MONK'S TOOTH. Ely.

DOG. Emblem of St. Roche; it symbolised fidelity and loyalty. It appears in many hunting scenes, and is generally portrayed as a smooth hound, with drooping ears.

DOCTOR AND PATIENT. Malvern.

DOLPHIN. Emblem of love and social feeling, also of diligence. The badge of Fitzjames, Warden of Merton College, 1482-1507, afterwards Bishop of Lincoln. Durham Cathedral.

DOMESTIC SCENE. Ely; Lincoln; Worcester; Boston; Whalley; Beverley.

  ,,   DISTURBANCE. Sherborne; Stratford; Chester; Bristol; Beverley; Durham Castle; Westminster.

DONYNGTON (ARMS). Beverley.

DRAGON. The emblem of Sin. In all ages this has been a favourite subject with artists, and there are some splendidly-carved examples. The dragon figures in many legends, especially those of German origin.

DULCIMER. A sort of hand-organ. Ely.

EAGLE. The symbol of power and generosity, emblem of the Ascension, and the attribute of St. John the Evangelist. Sometimes it holds a serpent, to signify victory over sin; sometimes a fish, the emblem of baptism. An eagle with two heads is the attribute of the prophet Elisha, referring to his petition for a "double portion of the Spirit." Whalley; All Souls' College; Boston.

  ,,   AND CHILD. The Lathom legend. Worcester; Whalley; Manchester.

  ,,   ON RABBIT. New College; St. Nicholas, Lynn.

ELEPHANT. The earliest-known carved example is at Exeter, and is more true to nature than many more recent ones, but the hocks are turned the wrong way. The first live elephant was brought to England in 1255, a few years later. There was a popular notion that the animal could not kneel down. Shakespeare makes Ulysses say, "The elephant hath joints, but none for courtesy; his legs are legs for necessity, not for flexure." Exeter; Cartmel.

ELEPHANT AND CASTLE. The arms of the city of Coventry. Guillim, the old herald, traces the origin of this design to the use of the animal in warfare, as described in Maccabees, chap. vi., 37: "And upon them were strong towers of wood that " covered every beast, which were fastened thereon with instruments; and upon " every one were thirty-two men that fought in them, and the Indian that ruled " him." St. Katharine's; Gloucester; Windsor; St. Mary's, Beverley; Manchester; Beverley Minster.

FALCON SEIZING DUCK. St. Katharine's; Worcester; Winchester College; Chester.

FALCON AND FETTERLOCK. The badge of the House of York. Hemington ; All Souls' ; Ludlow.

FIGHT BETWEEN CAMEL AND DRAGON. Lincoln ; Ripon.

    ,,   ,,   KNIGHT AND GIANT. Gloucester.

    ,,   ,,   LION AND DRAGON. Exeter; Sutton Courteney; Lincoln; Worcester; Gloucester; Ripon; Norwich; Gayton; Nantwich; Chester; Carlisle; Manchester; Beverley; &c.

    ,, BETWEEN MAN AND DRAGON. Norwich; Christchurch; Durham Castle; Beverley.

    ,,   ,,   CAMEL AND UNICORN. Manchester.

    ,,   ,,   LION AND GRIFFIN. Ripon.

    ,,   ,,   MAN AND WODEHOUSE. Christchurch.

    ,,   ,,   TWO WODEHOUSES. Chester.

    ,,   ,,   WODEHOUSE AND MONSTER. Manchester.

    ,,   ,,   WODEHOUSE AND BASILISK. Faversham.

FLEUR-DE-LYS. The arms of France, also the badge of Edward III. and Henry VII. Chester ; Lincoln.

FLUTE PLAYER. Faversham.

FOX AND GEESE. Winchester; Ely; Hereford; Gloucester; Fairford; Wellingborough; Norwich; Boston; Ripon; Faversham; Magdalen College; Beverley; &c.

    ,, AND GRAPES. Chester; Faversham.

    ,, FEIGNING DEATH. Chester.

    ,, AND STORK. Chester.

    ,, AND HOUNDS. Ripon; Beverley.

    ,, RIDING COCK. Westminster.

    ,, RIDING DOG. Manchester.

    ,, ABOUT TO BE HANGED. Bristol.

    ,, HANGED BY GEESE. Sherborne; St. Mary's, Beverley; Nantwich; Boston; Bristol; Beverley.

    ,, PREACHING. Ely; Cartmel; Etchingham; Gresford; Boston; St. Mary's, Beverley; Nantwich; Bristol; Windsor; Ripon; Beverley; Stowlangcroft.

FRIARS are distinguished from monks by the form of their habit and capuces, and by the knotted cords with which they are girt. Sherborne; St. Mary's, Beverley; &c.

GARDENER. Malvern.

GLOVES, TWO-FINGERED. Worcester; Winchester College.

GOAT. Winchester College; Passenham.

GOOD SHEPHERD. Winchester College.

GOOSE. The attribute of St. Martin, on account of its discovering the Saint, when, in timid modesty, he hid himself on being elected a Bishop. Beverley. It also relates to the legend of St. Werburgh. Chester.

GRANDISON (ARMS). Ottery St. Mary.

P

GRIFFIN. An heraldic animal, half eagle, half lion, denoting strength and swift-
ness, the emblem of vigilance; the ancient crest of the city of London.
Chichester; Lincoln; Chester; Carlisle; St. Mary's, Beverley; Ripon;
Beverley.

„   AND WOLF. Hereford.

GRIMACE-MAKER. Winchester; Ely; Sherborne; Stratford; Beverley.

GRINDING CORN. Ely; Beverley.

GUIGE. A strap of leather by which the shield of a soldier was hung over his shoulder
when not in use. Boston.

GYPCIÈRE. A purse or wallet made of leather, velvet or silk, either plain or embroidered;
sometimes a dagger was hung through it, a fashion introduced in Edward III.'s
time. The pickpockets of the period were known as "cut-purses," from the
method by which they obtained these pouches. *Hamlet* calls his uncle the
"cut-purse of the empire."

HAWKING. The sport chiefly of the nobility and gentry. Worcester; Ludlow; Beverley.

HARE (see Rabbit).

„   IN ITS FORM. Magdalen College.

HARPIES. Fabulous creatures, representing the winds and tempests; they have the
bodies of females, with the wings and feet of vultures. Their faces are sometimes beautiful, but cruel and vindictive. Winchester; Hereford.

HARP. The badge of Ireland, emblem of St. David, St. Cecilia, and St. Dunstan.
Chichester; Lincoln.

HARROW. Symbol for March. Ripple.

HAY-MAKING. Brampton.

HEAD-DRESS, HORNED. Minster; Swynbrook; Ludlow.

HEDGEHOG. Cartmel.

HELL-MOUTH. Usually represented as a monster's wide-open jaws, with sharp teeth,
into which demons thrust the lost souls. Ludlow; Gayton; Bristol.

HELM, MANTLED. Hemington; Boston.

HEN AND CHICKENS. Symbol of Spring, a device adopted by James III. of Scotland,
1460. Beverley.

HEROD AND HERODIAS. Ely.

HORSE. Magdalen College; Faversham; Durham Cathedral.

„   AND PORTCULLIS. Sir Yvain, according to a romance of the thirteenth century,
was in hot pursuit of a knight, and galloped after him over the drawbridge of
a castle; the portcullis dropping on his unfortunate steed, cut it in half. A
damsel named Lurit came to the knight's rescue and enabled him to escape
through a side door. Lincoln; Chester; Boston; New College.

HUNTING SCENES. Worcester; Ely; Sherborne; Norwich; St. Nicholas, Lynn; Boston;
Chester; Manchester; Beverley; &c.

ISLE OF MAN (ARMS). Manchester.

INFULÆ. Pendant ornaments on each side of a bishop's mitre. Ludlow; Boston.

JESSE, TREE OF. A vine, the emblem of spiritual fruitfulness, bearing on its numerous stems the portraits of the various persons mentioned in St. Matthew, chap. i., tracing the genealogy of Christ. St. Michael's, Coventry.

JONAH. Ripon.

JUDGMENT DAY. Lincoln; Gayton.

KING BETWEEN TWO BIRDS OR GRIFFINS. Lincoln; Gloucester; Chester; St. Mary's, Beverley; Darlington. ·

,, AND WODEHOUSE. All Souls' College; St. Mary's, Beverley.

KNIGHT OF THE SWAN. Exeter.

KNIGHTS IN COMBAT. Lincoln; Worcester; Malpas.

LAMB, THE PASCHAL. Passenham.

LANGLEY (ARMS). Darlington; Auckland.

LION. The attribute of St. Mark and St. Jerome, the symbol of sovereignty and power; a very favourite subject. Chichester; Lincoln; Fordham; Ripon; Manchester; &c.

,, COWARD. Chester; Durham Cathedral.

,, MAN ON CHAINED. Chester.

,, AND UNICORN. Beverley; Windsor.

,, WITH PAW ON MAN. Beverley.

,, ON MONKEY. Ripon.

LIRIPIPE. The long tail of a hood, frequently worn. Gloucester; Leighton Buzzard; Christchurch, &c.

MAGDALEN COLLEGE (ARMS). Magdalen.

MAGI, ADORATION OF. Lincoln.

,, OR SHEPHERDS. Gloucester.

MAN IN THE MOON. Ripple.

,, WHEELING WOMAN IN BARROW. Ripon; Durham Castle; Beverley.

MANSTON (ARMS). Minster.

MARYS, THE THREE. Gayton.

MERMAID. The most universal subject in misericord carving. The one at Chichester is the earliest and most pleasing in her extreme simplicity. The one at Westminster is the latest and least successful. The symbol of earthly pleasures which beguile their votaries from the path of virtue. Chichester; Lincoln; Winchester; Cartmel; Hereford; Malvern; All Souls'; Bakewell; Malpas; Bristol; Carlisle; Ludlow; Durham Castle; Westminster; Durham Cathedral; &c.

MERMAN. Malvern; Chichester Hospital.

MILKING. Beverley.

MITRE. Boston; St. Margaret's, Lynn; Ludlow.

MORSE. A brooch or buckle which fastens the cloak of a bishop. Ludlow.

MOSES AND AARON. Worcester.

MOWER. Malvern; Worcester; Brampton.

NEBUCHADNEZZAR. Exeter.

NOAH AND ARK. Ely.

NUN. Winchester; Higham Ferrers; Boston; Swine; &c.

OSTRICH. Exeter; Westminster.

OSTRICH FEATHERS. The badge of the Prince of Wales, the Heir-apparent. Ludlow; All Souls' College; Christchurch.

OWL. Winchester; Ely; Hemington; Boston; Ludlow; Ripon; Norwich; All Souls'; Christchurch; &c.

PASSION. The instruments of the Passion were commonly placed within a shield. Chester.

PEACOCK. Symbol of the Resurrection. New College; Durham Cathedral.

PELICAN. Symbol of maternal devotion and charity. She is usually depicted as feeding her young from her own breast, a proceeding described in heraldry as "in her piety." Ely; St. Katharine's; Lincoln; Winchester College; Cartmel; Gloucester; Carlisle; Boston; Walpole St. Peter's; &c.

PHŒNIX. Symbol of the Resurrection. Westminster.

PIG TEACHING YOUNG TO DANCE. Boston; Ripon; Richmond; Manchester; Beverley.

"   "   "   READ. Manchester.

"   AND LITTER. Winchester; Worcester; Chester.

"   RIDDEN BY BOY. Beverley.

"   PLAYING HARP. Manchester; Beverley; Durham.

"   "   BAGPIPES. Ripon; Durham Castle; Richmond; Westminster.

"   KILLED AND CUT-UP. Ripple; Bristol.

PLOUGHING. Lincoln.

PLOVER. Higham Ferrers.

PIPE AND TABOR. Generally used by mountebanks. Chichester; Hereford.

PORTCULLIS. The badge of the House of Tudor.

POSTURE-MAKER, OR TUMBLER. Chichester; Winchester; Hemington; All Souls'; Magdalen College; Christchurch.

QUINTAIN. Bristol.

QUOITS. Chester.

RABBIT'S OR HARE'S REVENGE. Manchester.

RABBIT PLAYING. Christchurch; Beverley.

"   RIDING HOUND. Worcester.

RATS HANGING CAT. Malvern.

REAPING. Worcester; Ripple; Brampton.

RESURRECTION, THE. Lincoln.

RED RIDING HOOD. Chester.

RHINOCEROS. Windsor.

RICHARD I. AND LION (see Samson).

ROSE IN GLORY, or *en soleil*. The badge of Edward IV. and Edward VI. Windsor.

ROSE. A badge borne by several kings; Edward I. was the earliest. Henry IV., Edward IV., and Henry VII. also adopted it.

RETURNED STALLS. Those which face the east. To "return" in architecture means to continue a piece of work in a different or opposite direction.

SAGITTARIUS. The badge of King Stephen; symbol for November. Exeter.

ST. ALBANS (ARMS). Leighton Buzzard.

ST. GEORGE'S CROSS. The arms of the city of London. Manchester.

ST. GEORGE AND THE DRAGON. Lincoln; Norwich; Stratford; Windsor; Whalley; St. Mary's, Beverley; Durham Castle.

ST. JOHN THE EVANGELIST. Generally represented writing his Gospel, or bearing a chalice from which a serpent issues, in allusion to the poisoned cup which was given him to drink. He was put into a cauldron of boiling oil, from which he escaped unhurt. Lincoln.

ST. JOHN THE BAPTIST, HIS EXECUTION. Ely.

ST. GILES THE HERMIT. The patron of beggars and cripples. He was accidentally wounded in the knee by an arrow by the King of France, who was hunting near his cell. The saint would not allow himself to be cured, and became a cripple; he was nourished by a hind who was generally represented near him. Ely.

ST. LUKE. The patron saint of artists; sometimes represented with painting materials near him. His attribute is an ox. Cockington.

ST. MARK. Generally accompanied by a winged lion. The patron saint of Venice. St. Gregory, Norwich; Christchurch.

ST. MARTIN was originally a soldier, and when riding one day in the winter met a half-clad beggar. He cut his military cloak in half, and gave a portion to the beggar. Ely.

ST. MATTHEW THE EVANGELIST. Represented as an old man with a beard; a cherub; or man's head with wings; sometimes with a purse, a spear, or a carpenter's rule or square. Cockington; St. Gregory, Norwich; Christchurch.

ST. MICHAEL AND DRAGON. Gloucester.

ST. NICHOLAS (ARMS). Minster.

ST. URSULA. A British princess who, with 11,000 virgins, was martyred at Cologne; sometimes represented with a crowd of small figures under the folds of her mantle, which she holds over them. Gayton (?).

ST. VERONICA. A woman who wiped the perspiration from the face of Christ on his way to Calvary, with a napkin, which thereupon received the impress of his features; a somewhat daring attempt to represent this in wood is at Higham Ferrers.

ST. WERBURGH was Prioress at Weedon, Northamptonshire, when the country was visited by flocks of wild geese, which did great damage to the crops. The Prioress commanded the geese to come to her house; they obeyed, and were impounded for the night. In the morning the Saint pardoned them, and gave them their liberty, on condition that they left the crops alone. During the night, however, a servant kept one of the geese, which was cooked and eaten.

The flock, missing one of their number, returned to St. Werburgh, and complained ; she found out what had happened, prayed over the bones of the goose, which received life, and the bird rejoined its comrades. The Saint went afterwards to Chester. Chester.

SALMON. Christchurch.

SAMSON, OR RICHARD I. The numerous stories of heroes of romance who have killed lions in single combat, with only natural weapons, make it difficult to identify the characters. Chichester; Ely; Worcester; Lincoln; Sherborne; Chester; Nantwich; Boston; Windsor; Bristol; Westminster.

„ AND DELILAH. Gloucester.

„ AND GATES OF GAZA. Ripon.

SARACEN'S HEADS. Rothwell.

SCHOOLMASTER AND BOYS. Sherborne; Norwich; Boston.

SCRIPTURAL SUBJECTS. Adam and Eve, Abraham, Absalom, David and Goliath, the Good Shepherd, Herod, Jonah, Judgment Day, Magi, Moses and Aaron, Samson, Solomon's Judgment (see under various headings).

SEPULCHRE AND ANGELS. Chester.

SEVEN DEADLY SINS. New College.

SHOES. The toes are usually square; long-pointed shoes were first worn in the fourteenth century. New College, &c.

SHOEING THE GOOSE. A proverbial expression found in Rabelais. Whalley; Bristol; Beverley.

SHEEP SHEARING. Beverley.

SOLOMON, JUDGMENT OF. Worcester; Beverley.

SOUTHAMPTON (ARMS). Christchurch.

SNAILS. Windsor.

SPHINX. Worcester.

SPIES IN CANAAN. Ripon; Beverley.

SPINNING. Winchester; Ely; Worcester; Fairford; Minster; New College.

SQUIRREL AND FIGURES. Bristol.

„   „ FRUIT. Winchester; Durham Cathedral.

STORK. Chester; Beverley.

SUN IN GLORY. Ripple.

SWAN. Exeter; Windsor; Leighton Buzzard; Stratford; Higham Ferrers; Bishop's Stortford; All Souls'; Ludlow; Magdalen.

SWELF. A rich merchant of Worcester, who went once a year to the Bishop to obtain absolution for his sins (in the same way as people, fond of good living, in these days pay an annual visit to Buxton). At last the Bishop advised him to become a monk, and thus avoid further temptation. Swelf promised to consider the matter, but could not bring his mind to it ; on his next visit, the Bishop declared that, whether he liked it or not, he should become a monk. In process of time, the prophecy came true, and Swelf adopted monastic life in the Priory of Malvern. But he contrived to secrete a portion of his beloved treasure, and only on his death-bed would he surrender it, with the view of obtaining full absolution for his past life. One of the carvings at Malvern is said to represent this incident.

SWINEHERD AND PIGS. Lincoln; Worcester; Malvern.

TABOR. The old name for the Drum (see Pipe).

TAIT (ARMS). Beverley.

THISTLES, MAN CUTTING. Malvern.

THRESHING. Ely; Tufton Street; Westminster.

TRADES. Carver, Weaver, Butcher (see).

TRIPLE FACE. May be a device representing the Trinity, the Three Wise Men of the East, or it may be merely the carver's own quaint conceit. Cartmel; Faversham. A quadruple face is at Worcester.

UNICORN. A fabulous animal of great ferocity. Its form was that of a horse or antelope, with a single horn, and a long tufted tail; the horn was the most powerful antidote to poison, and was highly valued. The "horn of Windsor" is referred to by writers as one of the chief curiosities of Windsor Castle. This precious article was, in all probability, the long twisted tusk of the Narwhal, which was brought by sailors from the northern seas. It lived in forests, and was so wary that no man could succeed in approaching it; but if a pure maiden came near its haunts, it would come to her, lay its head in her lap, and allow the hunters to take it. It is to be hoped that few maidens consented so basely to betray the creature's confidence! It was the emblem of purity, and the Incarnation, the attribute of the Virgin Mary, St. Agatha, and St. Justinian, and in heraldry was adopted as a "supporter" by James IV. of Scotland. Lincoln; Stratford; Boston; Manchester; Beverley.

Another method of capture adopted by hunters, and also by the lion, its time-honoured antagonist, was to take shelter near a tree, and when the Unicorn charged in great fury, to slip behind the trunk, when the horn, piercing the bark, held the poor animal captive. *Decius* declares that *Cæsar*
> " loves to hear
> That unicorns may be betrayed with trees,
> And bears with glasses, elephants with holes,
> Lions with toils, and men with flatterers."

This method of capture is shown at Cartmel.

VALENTINE AND ORSON, according to a romance of the fifteenth century, were twin sons of Alexander of Constantinople, born in a forest near Orleans. Orson, one of the babies, was carried off and brought up by a bear; while his mother went in search of him, the other brother was found and taken by King Pippin, his uncle. Orson grew up a wild man of the woods, and is probably the original of many of the "wodehouse" subjects. His brother Valentine, taken to court, became a knight, and married the "Green Knight's" sister. Their accidental meeting is shown at St. Mary's, Beverley. Gloucester; Ripon; Chester.

Vineyard. Gloucester ; Westminster.

Virgin and Child. Chester.

    ,,   crowned. Lincoln ; Gloucester ; Chester.

    ,,   Assumption of. Lincoln.

Weaver. Brampton.

Weights (Heraldic). Beverley.

Whale. Bishop's Stortford.

Windmill. Windsor.

Window. New College.

Winter Scene. Worcester ; Ripple ; Ripon ; Beverley.

Wodehouse. A name given by heralds to a wild man of the woods, who is usually
clothed in skins and armed with a club. He was the satyr of the Middle Ages.
See *Valentine.* Winchester ; Lincoln ; Windsor ; Hereford ; Norwich ; Boston ;
Faversham ; Beverley ; Westminster.

Wrestling. Hereford ; Gloucester ; Windsor ; Chester ; Norwich ; Bristol.

TOPOGRAPHICAL LIST.

—

BEDFORDSHIRE	St. Paul's, Bedford; Leighton Buzzard; Nuthill; Eddlesborough; Biggleswade.
BERKSHIRE	Fyfield: Wantage; Windsor: St. George's Chapel; Sutton Courteney.
BUCKS	North Marston; Aylesbury.
CAMBRIDGESHIRE	Ely; Fordham; Gamlingay; Isleham; Landbeach; Milton; Soham; Over; Cambridge: King's College; Architectural Museum; Walpole St. Peter's.
CHESHIRE	Chester Cathedral; Nantwich.
CORNWALL	St. German's.
CUMBERLAND	Carlisle.
DERBYSHIRE	Bakewell; Tideswell.
DEVONSHIRE	Exeter Cathedral; Ottery St. Mary.
DORSETSHIRE	Sherborne; Wimborne; Charmouth.
DURHAM	Durham Cathedral and Castle; Darlington; Bishop Auckland.
ESSEX	Castle Hedingham.
GLOUCESTERSHIRE	Bristol; Fairford; Gloucester Cathedral.
HAMPSHIRE	Winchester Cathedral; Christchurch; Winchester College Chapel.
HEREFORDSHIRE	Canon Pryor: Hereford: Cathedral, All Saints'; Ledbury.
HERTFORDSHIRE	Anstey; Bishop's Stortford; Wheathampstead.
HUNTS	Brampton, now in Cambridge Museum.
KENT	Aldington; Cliffe-at-Hor; Herne; Faversham; Maidstone: All Saints'; Minster; Sandwich: St. Clement's; Throwley; Wingate.
LANCASHIRE	Garstang; Lancaster; Manchester Cathedral; Middleton; Halsall; Whalley.
LINCOLNSHIRE	Boston; Lincoln Cathedral.
MIDDLESEX	Henry VII.'s Chapel, Westminster; St. Katharine's Hospital; Tufton Street Museum.
NORFOLK	Aylsham; Binham; Blakeney; Castle Acre; Cawston; Cley-next-the-Sea; East Lexham; Grimston; Lynn: St. Margaret, St. Nicholas; Litcham; Norwich: Cathedral, St. Andrew, St. Gregory, St. Swithin; North Walsham; Ranworth; Salle; Tilney; Trunch; &c.

Q

NOTTINGHAMSHIRE	· ·	Southwell.
NORTHAMPTONSHIRE	· ·	Doddington; Gayton; Hennington; Higham Ferrers; Holdenby; Irthlingborough; Peterborough Cathedral; Passenham; Rothwell; Tansor; Wellingborough.
NORTHUMBERLAND	· ·	Hexham.
OXFORDSHIRE	·· ·	Bampton; Kidlington; Oxford: All Souls', New College, Magdalen, Lincoln; Swynbrook.
RUTLAND · ·	·	Stamford: Browne's Hospital.
SHROPSHIRE	· ·	Ludlow; Tong.
SOMERSETSHIRE ·	·	Wells Cathedral; North Cadbury; Worle.
STAFFORDSHIRE ·	·	Enville; Penkridge.
SUFFOLK · ·	·	Cockfield; Lavenham; Norton; Southwold; Stowlangcroft; Sudbury: St. Gregory.
SURREY · ·	·	Beddington; Lingfield.
SUSSEX · ·	·	Broadwater; Chichester: Cathedral, St. Mary's Hospital; Etchingham; West Tarring.
WARWICKSHIRE ·	·	Coventry: Holy Trinity; Stratford-on-Avon.
WILTSHIRE · ·	·	Mere; Salisbury: Cathedral, St. Thomas.
WORCESTERSHIRE	·	Great Malvern; Ripple; Worcester Cathedral.
YORKSHIRE · ·	· ·	Beverley: Minster, St. Mary; Hackness; Hemingborough; Richmond; Ripon; Rotherham; Swine; Wakefield.
WALES · ·	· ·	Bangor; Beaumaris; Gresford; St. David's.
SCOTLAND · ·	· ·	Dunblane Cathedral.
IRELAND · ·	· ·	Cork Cathedral; Limerick: St. Mary.

CHRONOLOGICAL LIST,

AS FAR AS CAN BE ASCERTAINED.

Exeter	· · · ·	1244	St. Mary, Beverley ·	· ·	1445
Chichester Cathedral·	· ·	13th cent.	Windsor · · ·	· ·	1450
Winchester Cathedral	· ·	13th ,,	Swynbrook, Oxon. ·	· ·	1450
Sutton Courteney	· ·	13th ,,	Throwley, Kent	· ·	1450
Salisbury Cathedral ·	· ·	13th ,,	Fairford, Gloucestershire ·	·	1460
Ottery St. Mary	· ·	1350	Cawston, Norfolk ·	· ·	1460
Fordham ·	· · ·	1350	Rotherham	· ·	1480
Ely Cathedral ·	· · ·	1350	New College, Oxon ·	· ·	1480
Soham	· · · (?)	1350	Ripon Cathedral	· ·	1490
St. Katharine, London	· ·	1350	Gamlingay	· · ·	15th cent.
Lincoln Cathedral ·	· ·	1370	Bakewell, Derbyshire	· ·	15th ,,
Boston ·	· · ·	1375	Kidlington, Oxon ·	·	15th ,,
Hereford Cathedral ·	· ·	1380	Salle, Norfolk ·	· ·	15th ,,
Hemington, Northampton·	·	1380	Swine, Yorkshire	· ·	15th ,,
Rothwell, Northampton · (?)		1380	North Walsham, Norfolk ·	·	15th ,,
Irthlingborough, Northampton ·		1380	St. Margaret, Lynn ·	·	15th ,,
Wellingborough, Northampton ·		1390	St. Nicholas, Lynn ·	·	15th ,,
Higham Ferrers	· ·	14th cent.	Carlisle Cathedral ·	·	15th ,,
Worcester Cathedral·	· ·	14th ,,	Chester Cathedral	· ·	15th ,,
Ripple ·	· · ·	14th ,,	Norwich Cathedral ·	·	15th ,,
St. Mary's, Lancaster	· ·	14th ,,	Ludlow · · ·	·	15th ,,
Leighton Buzzard	· ·	14th ,,	Gayton, Northants ·	·	15th ,,
Sherborne Minster ·	· ·	14th ,,	Bedford · · ·	·	15th ,,
Gloucester Cathedral	· ·	14th ,,	Faversham, Kent ·	·	15th ,,
Winchester College ·	· ·	14th ,,	Peterborough Cathedral ·	·	15th ,,
Cartmel, Lancashire ·	· ·	14th ,,	Richmond, Yorks ·	·	1500
Brampton, Hunts. ·	· ·	14th ,,	Aylsham, Norfolk ·	·	1507
Malvern ·	· · ·	1400	Manchester Cathedral ·	·	1508
Nuthill, Berks. ·	· ·	1405	Christchurch, Hants ·	·	1510
Chichester Hospital ·	· ·	1407	Durham Castle ·	·	1510
Minster, Kent ·	· ·	1410	Westminster Abbey ·	·	1510
Beddington, Surrey ·	· ·	1410	Beverley, Yorks ·	·	1520
Maidstone, Kent	· ·	1410	King's College, Camb. ·	·	1534
Walpole St. Peter's, Camb.	·	1420	Wimborne, Dorset ·	·	1608
Tilney, Norfolk ·	· ·	1423	Passenham, Northants ·	·	1628
Whalley, Lancashire·	· ·	1435	Lincoln College, Oxford ·	·	1630
Bishop's Stortford ·	· ·	1420	Durham Cathedral ·	·	1660
All Souls', Oxford ·	· ·	1442			

www.ingramcontent.com/pod-product-compliance
Lightning Source LLC
Chambersburg PA
CBHW031341070726
47496CB00017B/1403